Heirloom
VEGETABLES

A HOME GARDENER'S GUIDE TO FINDING AND GROWING VEGETABLES FROM THE PAST

SUE STICKLAND

CONSULTANT: KENT WHEALY AT SEED SAVERS EXCHANGE

PHOTOGRAPHS BY DAVID CAVAGNARO

LEFT: *Traditional varieties of Alliums can be grown without difficulty in most climates, including red- or white-skinned onions, pearl onions and shallots, leeks, and many different types of garlic.*

FIRESIDE
Rockefeller Center
1230 Avenue of the Americas
New York, NY 10020

FIRESIDE and colophon are registered trademarks
of Simon & Schuster Inc.

Designed by Kitty Crossley
Edited by Charlie Ryrie
Part Two compiled by Charlie Ryrie

10 9 8 7 6 5 4 3 2 1

Library of Congress Cataloging-in-Publication Data
Stickland, Sue
        Heirloom vegetables : a home gardener's guide to finding and
growing vegetables from the past / Sue Stickland : foreword by Kent
Whealy : photographs by David Cavagnaro.
        p.   cm.
Includes biographical references (p. 5) and Index.
        ISBN 0-684-83807-9 (pbk.)
        1. Vegetables—Heirloom varieties. 2. Vegetable gardening.
I. Title
SB324.73.S75 1998   97–29441
635—dc21   CIP

Printed in Hong Kong

THE AUTHOR

Sue Stickland has worked as a professional gardener for 20 years. She was Head Gardener with the Henry Doubleday Research Association (HDRA) when they set up their organic gardens in Central England, and there became involved with the HDRA's Heritage Vegetable collection. She is an established author, writing books and articles on organic gardening and related topics, and she presented a popular Channel 4 TV series on organic gardening.

THE CONSULTANT

Kent Whealy founded the Seed Savers Exchange (SSE) with his wife Diane in 1975, and it has grown to be one of the most important international organizations for promoting and conserving the genetic diversity of the world's food crops. SSE's members maintain and distribute thousands of heirloom varieties, including crops kept by Native Americans and other traditional communities such as Mennonites and Amish. Kent is deeply involved in vital seed collecting expeditions in Eastern Europe and the former Soviet Union to help save the genetic heritage of those countries, which is also rapidly disappearing. Seed Savers Exchange started with just two varieties of garden seeds passed down through Diane's family for several generations; today SSE's seed bank contains 18,000 varieties of heirloom seeds, and 8,000 members in 14 countries exchange seeds, knowledge and traditions while keeping our garden seed heritage well and truly alive.

THE PHOTOGRAPHER

David Cavagnaro is a naturalist, plantsman, writer, and photographer whose words and pictures have appeared in books and magazines worldwide. Arriving at Seed Savers Exchange in Iowa 12 years ago, on a photographic assignment for *Organic Gardener* magazine, he was so inspired that he stayed to help. For 8 years he was the curator at the SSE gardens, and he probably knows more than anyone about their range of vegetables, having grown and photographed many of them.

PUBLISHER'S ACKNOWLEDGMENTS

Gaia Books would like to thank Kent and Diane Whealy at Seed Savers Exchange for their support and help; a very special thank you to David Cavagnaro and Joanie Shehan, without whose hospitality in Iowa in summer 1996 this book might never have happened; thanks to David also for his willingness to share information, and for his help in identification; and to Glenn Drowns for additional varietal identification.

Thanks to all the seed suppliers and individuals who willingly sent us masses of information, and often took the time to send personal letters and good wishes as well. Without all their work, this book could not exist.

Thanks to Colin Wilkin for his artwork on pages 22–23 and page 53; Charlie Ryrie for photographs on pages 90 and 95, and Lyn Bresler for preparing the Index.

CONTENTS

FOREWORD

The seeds planted each year by gardeners and farmers are living links in an unbroken chain reaching back into antiquity. We cannot possibly comprehend the magnitude of the history contained in these seeds in terms of what has gone before and what may potentially come after our brief involvement. Our Neolithic ancestors began domesticating plants 10,000 years ago with the simple act of replanting seeds that had been gathered for food. Whenever gardeners begin to save their own seeds, they also become part of this ancient tradition.

Because the United States and Canada are nations of immigrants, North American gardeners are blessed with an immense cornucopia of food crops. Gardeners and farmers from every corner of the world invariably brought along their best seeds when their families immigrated. Afraid these treasured seeds might be confiscated upon arrival, new immigrants often hid their seeds in the linings of suitcases, under the bands of hats and sewn into the hems of dresses. Seeds provided living memories of their former lives and ensured continued enjoyment of foods from the old country. This unique heritage of seeds was first brought over almost four centuries ago by passengers on the Mayflower, and is still arriving today with boat people and refugees from Laos, Cambodia, Haiti, and Cuba.

Many of the heirloom varieties that arrived with the great flood of immigrants during the 19th century are still being grown today by gardeners and farmers in isolated rural areas and ethnic enclaves across North America. Often these living heirlooms have been grown on the same farm by different generations of a family for 150 years or more. But economic conditions continue to force young people off the land in droves, and elderly gardeners often can find no-one to continue growing the family's seeds. As the older generation passes away, unless dedicated gardeners continue to replant their unique seeds, those outstanding strains become extinct. Future generations will never enjoy them and invaluable genetic characteristics are lost forever to gardeners and plant breeders.

In 1972 my wife's terminally ill grandfather entrusted us with seeds that his parents had brought from Bavaria to northeast Iowa in the 1800s. When Grandpa Ott passed away that winter, Diane and I knew that the survival of the family's seeds was up to us. About that same time, we read several articles by prominent geneticists – Jack Harlan, Garrison Wilkes, Erna Bennett – about the catastrophic potential of genetic erosion, warning of increasing epidemics and infestations if the breeding material for the food crops of the future continued to die out at such a rapid and alarming rate.

Diane and I immediately started trying to locate other families who were also keeping heirloom seeds, hoping to increase the genetic diversity available to gardeners growing healthy food for their families (43 million US families, about 40%, grow some part of their own food, and two-thirds of the world's people live on what they can grow). We soon discovered a vast, almost unknown genetic treasure quietly being maintained by elderly gardeners and farmers. Heirloom seeds are especially prevalent in isolated mountainous areas, such as the Ozarks, Smokies, and Appalachians, and also among traditional peoples such as the Mennonites, Amish and Native Americans. It became immediately apparent that these were excellent home garden varieties, often extremely flavorful, tender, and productive. Gardeners are continuously growing and comparing varieties: those that don't measure up are quickly discarded, certainly not maintained for 150 years or more. And over such long periods, many of these heirloom seeds had slowly developed resistances to local diseases and insects, and had gradually become well adapted to specific climates and soil conditions. This heritage of heirloom seeds, which vastly outnumbers the offerings of the entire garden seed industry in North America, had never been systematically collected.

Diane and I founded the Seed Savers Exchange in 1975. For more than two decades we have continued to locate gardeners keeping heirloom food crops, and have organized them into an annual seed exchange. Each January SSE publishes a yearbook that lists all of the seeds being offered by our members. In 1975 that network consisted of 29 members offering a few dozen varieties through a six-page newsletter, now there are 1,000 'listed members' offering nearly 12,000 rare varieties through the current 400-page *Seed Savers Yearbook* sent to 8,000 gardeners. Over the years SSE's members have distributed an estimated 750,000 samples of rare seeds that were unavailable commercially and were often on the verge of extinction.

In 1986 SSE purchased our 170-acre Heritage Farm, where permanent collections are maintained and displayed. Each summer 3,000 visitors tour nine large organic Preservation Gardens and the Historic Orchard, containing 700 19th century apples and 200 hardy grapes, and view herds of Ancient White Park cattle. The collection of seeds at Heritage Farm recently exceeded 18,000 varieties: 4,100 tomatoes, 3,600 beans, 1,200 peppers, 1,000 squash, 900 peas, 800 lettuces, 600 corns, 400 melons, 200 watermelons and 200 garlics. Every year the seeds of about 2,000 varieties are multiplied in the Preservation Gardens, processed and heat-sealed into foil packets, and stored in the basement of the office complex. Excess seeds

(beyond our grow-out needs) are then made available to SSE's members. SSE's genetic preservation efforts have been highly successful, even though our members have been collecting from a fragmented ethnic patchwork surrounded by almost completely mechanized agriculture. Other areas in the world are much richer in traditional food crops. For example, traditional agriculture in Eastern Europe and the former Soviet Union varies from unbroken to virtually destroyed, depending largely on the extent of Stalin's collectivization of Soviet farms. Some areas are extremely rich botanically, especially wet mountainous regions that were too rugged for the gigantic Soviet collective farms. In such areas, traditional agriculture reaches back unbroken with all seeds still produced by gardeners and farmers. But Western agricultural technology, plus American, Japanese and Dutch seeds, are currently flooding into even the most remote mountain villages, and fragile genetic resources are disappearing.

In 1992 SSE began developing Seed Savers International, a network of plant collectors in genetically rich Eastern European countries who are rescuing traditional food crops that are in danger of extinction. The project has required many trips to Eastern Europe and the former Soviet Union, to establish working relationships with scientists at the Gaterslaben seed bank in Eastern Germany, and the Vavilov Institute in St Petersburg. During the last four years SSI has funded plant collecting expeditions in Romania, Poland, on remote islands between Sicily and Tunisia, throughout Sardinia, through Uzbekistan and Kazakhstan, in areas of Russia and in western Ukraine and Belarus. Half of the resulting seeds is donated to the host country's seed bank; the other half is taken back to Gaterslaben or the Vavilov Institute, where scientists split the samples again and send a portion to Heritage Farm. The program has been highly successful, and for once there are no losers: the best plant collectors in the world have been able to continue collecting; endangered traditional seeds in genetically rich areas are being rescued; each country retains the use and benefits of its own genetic resources; and Heritage Farm provides a safe haven and valuable back-up for endangered foreign collections. Since 1993, seeds of 3,000 traditional vegetable varieties from 30 Eastern countries have arrived at Heritage Farm. These seeds are gradually being multiplied and evaluated, and then made available to SSE's members who provide further maintenance and distribution.

There are even some bright rays of hope emanating from the garden seed industry. Unlike the European Community, where massive self-inflicted losses were legislated with the Common Catalogue, similarly devastating losses in the US and Canada have resulted strictly from economic consolidation. Starting in 1981, SSE has compiled and published four editions of the *Garden Seed Inventory* – comprehensive source books listing all non-hybrid vegetable seeds still available by mail order in the US and Canada. The worst losses occurred a decade ago. Out of 230 seed companies inventoried in 1984, 54 went out of business or had been taken over by 1987. Fourteen years of statistics to 1994 document steady losses of about 6% of all non-hybrid vegetables each year. That's 84% in 14 years. SSE has been using profits from each edition of the *Garden Seed Inventory* to buy up endangered varieties while sources still exist.

The good news is that during 1991-94 1,794 entirely new varieties were introduced. Many are heirlooms being offered by small alternative and specialized seed companies, and even by some of SSE's largest members. But our statistics also show that a mere 21 companies introduced 50% of those new varieties, so these gains are extremely fragile and could be wiped out by the loss of just a few companies. Even so, it appears that two decades of effort by SSE to raise national awareness of preserving diversity is finally having a national impact.

There has never been a more exciting time to be a gardener! You have access to thousands of heirloom varieties that have been rescued and maintained by excellent, dedicated, genetic preservation organizations like the SSE, Seeds of Diversity (Canada), Henry Doubleday Research Association (UK) and Arche Noah (Austria). Centuries of history (ours is short) are available for the choosing: pre-Columbian seeds grown by Native American tribes throughout North America; seeds brought over on the Mayflower; varieties grown by Thomas Jefferson in his gardens at Monticello; seeds carried by the Cherokee over the Trail of Tears (the infamous winter death march, 1838-39); and the best seeds from every corner of the world that immigrants and refugees have treasured, protected, and shared. Many remote areas of the former Communist world, where Westerners were not allowed for over 70 years, are slowly opening like creaky treasure chests. Be careful though, because the cruel irony is that much of this incredibly beautiful genetic richness is very close to dying out forever. The addictive fascination of varietal diversity can easily lead to a compelling sense of stewardship that could change your life. Welcome to the inspiring and fascinating world of heirloom seeds.

Kent Whealy

Kent Whealy · July 1997
Executive Director, Seed Savers Exchange, Decorah, Iowa.

PART

1

Variety,
the Essence of Life

❶

OUR VEGETABLE HERITAGE

ABOVE: *Potatoes come in many guises, and thousands of varieties exist, each with distinctive qualities and appearance.*

LEFT: *This small selection of European heirloom lettuces hints at the wide diversity of colors and leaf shapes.*

Dazzling displays of supermarket vegetables, lit brightly and scrubbed clean, deceive us with their size and color. A display in a New York store will be almost identical to one in London, or in Paris or in Stockholm – and it will be much the same in January as in June. You will see the same types of vegetables, and they are likely to be exactly the same varieties. Tomatoes are most often round and red; potatoes are either 'reds' or 'whites', and a carrot – well, a carrot is just a carrot. Seasonal produce and local varieties appear to have vanished, and with them choice, and very often taste.

If you can grow your own vegetables, you are immediately better off. You have to harvest seasonally, and seed catalogs give you more choice than any supermarket shelf. However, you need to search out your suppliers carefully; the continuing drive for homogeneity means major seed companies offer far shorter lists than a few decades ago. Moreover, many of the new entries are modern hybrids, with few significant differences between varieties, and with qualities which may be quite irrelevant to a gardener. Conventional seed suppliers are rarely small local businesses any more, but have increasingly become part of large corporations.

Yet an amazing diversity of vegetables does still exist, in ranges of shape, size, color, cooking quality, and taste that most of us have never dreamt of, and with differences in cold-tolerance, harvest times, and resistance to pests and diseases that are of immense value to gardeners and growers. Only a handful of these varieties can be found in shops, or even seed catalogs, today.

Potatoes are one of the best examples of this significant impoverishment; they are a staple crop of world importance, and Europe and America are among the chief producers. However, most commercial potato growers in these countries will plant just two or three varieties each year, and there is a good chance that neighbouring farmers will be planting the same ones. In the UK in the early 1990s, the ten most commonly grown potatoes occupied around 70 per cent of the total area put down to the crop. These same varieties are obviously the ones that are most likely to be found in shops and supermarkets, and inevitably they are going to be the ones most likely to be sold as seed potatoes to gardeners. This ever narrowing base is despite the fact that at least 230 varieties were available in 1996 through US and Canadian catalogs, and 150 varieties via UK

TOMATOES

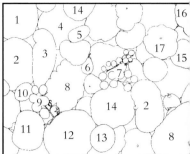

1. Pink Brandywine

2. Evergreen

3. Opalka Paste

4. Pineapple

5. Red Plum

6. Red Pear

7. Red Currant

8. Ribbed Zapotec

9. Broad Ripple Yellow Currant

10. Yellow Pear

11. Golden Queen

12. Big Rainbow

13. Tigerella

14. White Snowball

15. Stuffer

16. Great White

17. Costoluto Genovese

seed suppliers. Many more are in the hands of amateur collectors and seed saving groups in their respective countries.

These monocultures in developed countries contrast strongly with the traditional ways of peasant farmers in the Andes. Here it is not uncommon to find at least 45 distinct potato varieties growing in one valley, and it has been estimated that Andean farmers cultivate some 3,000 different varieties in total, potatoes of varied shapes and a whole spectrum of colors from black to bright yellow.

The tomato is another crop with seemingly endless diversity – so often reduced by commercial growers and supermarkets to smooth round red fruits. Most of us have tasted smaller, sweet cherry tomatoes, and seen the occasional yellow tomato or fleshy beefsteak type on the shelves of some stores, or among the many new F1 hybrids in popular seed catalogs. But this is just the tip of a largely hidden iceberg of diversity. Tomatoes can be red, pink, orange, yellow, black, green or white, and streaks are not uncommon. They may be egg-shaped or

ABOVE: *Originating in Russia, Black Krim tomatoes are thin-skinned, sweet and incredibly juicy.*

pear-shaped, or have ridges and bulges. Some are very solid and others almost hollow, they may be bitter or sweet, and they have numerous different uses in the kitchen.

Size, shape, color, and taste are a few of the obvious ways in which tomatoes can vary. Other characteristics, such as the ability to set (form fruit) in cold conditions, or resistance to fungal diseases, are equally important to growers and gardeners, but can easily go unnoticed. In the mid 1990s well over 600 varieties were commercially available via seed suppliers in the US and Canada, 150 in the UK, over 400 offered by the US network Seed Savers Exchange, and 2,500 varieties kept as seed in the gene bank in Gatersleben, Germany.

This vast diversity of crops has co-evolved over hundreds of years, together with the people who cultivated and used them. It is fitting that we should regard them as our heritage, and look upon the individual varieties as heirlooms – something precious beyond monetary value. The problem with heirloom vegetables is that, unlike gold watches or bibles, plants and their seeds have a short life. In order to survive they have to be grown and cared for.

Many old varieties still in existence are, quite literally, family heirlooms, their seeds handed down from one generation to the next, never coming into the hands of the commercial seed companies. At one time, saving seeds and passing them on was a matter of survival – otherwise there would be no seed to sow the following year, no crop to harvest and no food to eat. American Indians, or peasant farmers in any culture, would have taken this for granted. However, by the second half of the 20th century, only a small minority of growers were saving their own seed; most relied instead on the seed companies. Fortunately, a few families and communities have carried on their traditional seed saving ways, and a large number

BOOTHBY'S BLOND
CUCUMBER

The distinctive cucumber, Boothby's Blond, was grown for several generations by the Boothby family in Maine, but only became commercially available in the mid 1990s, when it was taken up by a couple of small US seed companies with an interest in old varieties.

Short, oval fruits have warty creamy-yellow skin and very sweet and delicate flesh.

Boothby's Blond is ideal for cooler climates, as long as it is grown in a sunny position.

SUMMER SQUASH

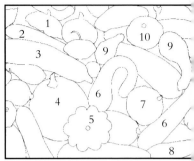

1. Bennings Green Tint
2. Golden Zucchini
3. Bulgarian Summer
4. Ronde de Nice
5. White Bush Scallop
6. Cocozelle
7. Mandan
8. Caserta
9. Early Summer Crookneck
10. Weisser Patisson

of the old varieties do still exist. Many of these have a history that can be traced back well over a hundred years, others may date from early this century; all are valuable.

In the US, one important heirloom is a bronze-tinged leafy lettuce, Grandpa Admires (*see right*). It was the gift of seeds of this old variety that motivated the establishment of Seed Savers Exchange. A favourite UK heirloom is a crimson-flowered *fava* (broad) bean. An elderly lady, who had seen her father growing the beans throughout his life, passed on seeds to the Henry Doubleday seed saving group in 1978. Although crimson-flowered broad beans were recorded as long ago as 1778, and despite their value as food and ornament – the flowers are highly attractive – they never made it into commercial seed catalogs. Without such a donation they would have become extinct, along with their history and unique genetic make-up.

Some much-loved old varieties developed as the result of traditional plant breeding programs by small seed companies. Although not heirlooms in the sense of being kept alive by families, they are also vitally important. Many of them, such as Scarlet Emperor runner bean, or Golden Bantam corn, are now being labeled by seed merchants as inferior, and are at risk of being completely replaced by modern hybrids (*see page 41*).

In discovering traditional varieties, it is easy to get caught up in nostalgia and delve deeper and deeper into the past. But these plants are also a fundamental part of the future. Using the words 'heritage' and 'heirloom' recognizes that we are responsible for preserving the wealth of vegetable diversity that still exists – not by keeping them as museum pieces, but by growing them, using them, and passing them on.

GRANDPA ADMIRES (*above*)

George Admire was a civil war veteran born in 1822. In 1977 his granddaughter, 90-year-old Cloe Lowrey, gave some of his lettuce seed to Kent and Diane Whealy. This gift, added to two varieties of seeds passed down through generations of Diane's family, inspired the Whealys to set up Seed Savers Exchange, a network dedicated to preserving the genetic diversity of the world's food crops through saving heirlooms and endangered varieties.

ANDEAN POTATOES

In the Peruvian valleys, there is a potato variety covered in little knobs which the native people are said to call 'the potato that makes the young bride weep'. A new bride can be sent away if she is not nimble enough to peel one of these potatoes without slicing off a knob.

The origins of crops

Modern researchers do not always agree about the exact origins of individual crops, or where they were first developed. But the concept that crops have specific centers of diversity is an important one. These centers are nearly all in tropical or subtropical regions, often close to, and isolated by, mountains, lakes, and rivers. These regions have wide variations in soil type and climate, and usually encompass different peoples with varying needs, all factors which force different adaptations of the crops.

Most of our important crops came originally from the Near East, Northern China, and parts of Southern America, where there is an enormous genetic variation in the crops, and their wild relatives. Central Asia is thought to be the centre of origin of carrots, spinach, onion, peas, and broad beans (*Vicia spp*); South America is deemed the source of squashes, corn, potatoes, tomatoes, and French, runner, and lima beans (*Phaseolus spp*). Such areas are often referred to as Vavilov centers after the Russian scientist who first proposed the idea.

Secondary centers of diversity are typically regions where a crop was introduced very early on, and then had a chance to develop many varied forms. For example, many of our cultivated tomatoes originated in Mexico and Central America, yet the crop is descended from wild species from the Andes, where the greatest numbers of wild forms are still found. One theory suggests that tomatoes traveled to Mexico as a weed in corn crops.

Very few vegetables are indigenous to North America or Northern Europe. Most have been brought in by travelers – conquering armies, refugees, explorers, slaves, immigrants, missionaries, or even wildlife.

CROOKNECK SQUASH
(*CUCURBITA PEPO*)

Bulb-shaped squashes with narrow curved necks were amongst the first types of squash to be taken back to Europe from South America by the Spanish. Old varieties, such as Yellow Crookneck, are still grown today. These are summer squashes, best eaten fresh from the vine when the fruits are no longer than 6 inches. The skin becomes bumpy and warted as the fruits get larger.

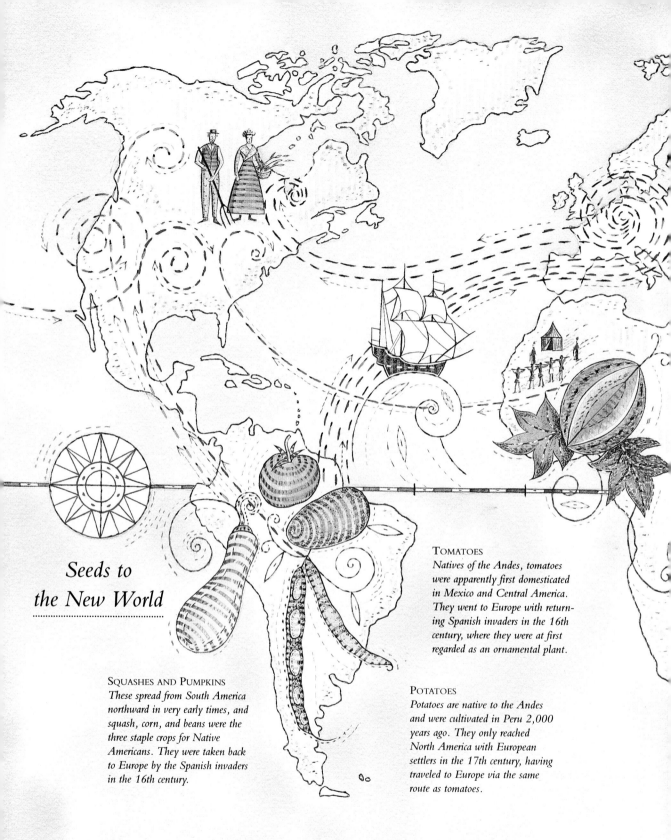

Seeds to the New World

TOMATOES

Natives of the Andes, tomatoes were apparently first domesticated in Mexico and Central America. They went to Europe with returning Spanish invaders in the 16th century, where they were at first regarded as an ornamental plant.

SQUASHES AND PUMPKINS

These spread from South America northward in very early times, and squash, corn, and beans were the three staple crops for Native Americans. They were taken back to Europe by the Spanish invaders in the 16th century.

POTATOES

Potatoes are native to the Andes and were cultivated in Peru 2,000 years ago. They only reached North America with European settlers in the 17th century, having traveled to Europe via the same route as tomatoes.

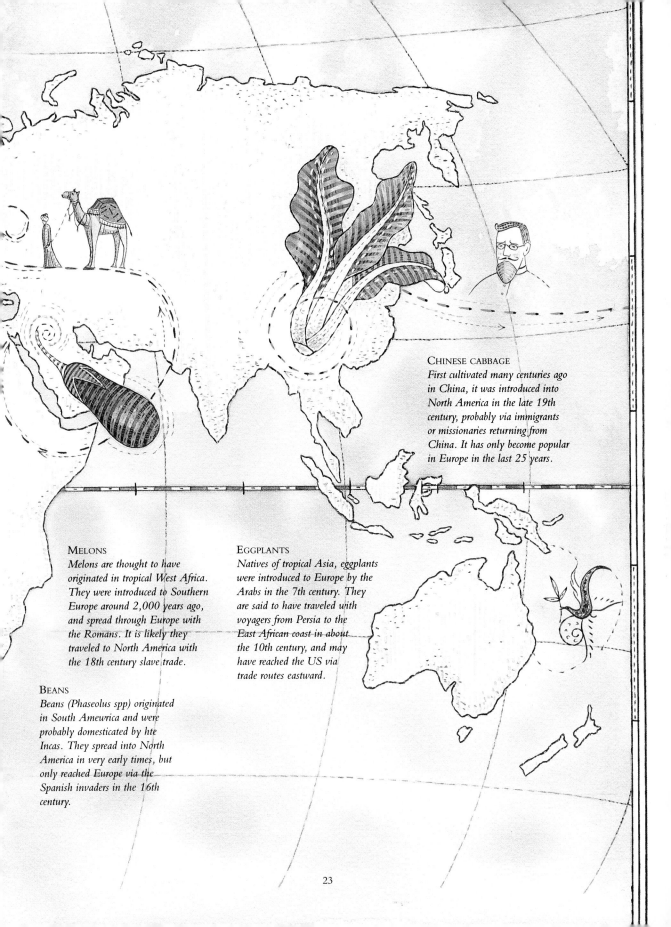

CHINESE CABBAGE
First cultivated many centuries ago in China, it was introduced into North America in the late 19th century, probably via immigrants or missionaries returning from China. It has only become popular in Europe in the last 25 years.

MELONS
Melons are thought to have originated in tropical West Africa. They were introduced to Southern Europe around 2,000 years ago, and spread through Europe with the Romans. It is likely they traveled to North America with the 18th century slave trade.

BEANS
Beans (Phaseolus spp) originated in South Amewrica and were probably domesticated by hte Incas. They spread into North America in very early times, but only reached Europe via the Spanish invaders in the 16th century.

EGGPLANTS
Natives of tropical Asia, eggplants were introduced to Europe by the Arabs in the 7th century. They are said to have traveled with voyagers from Persia to the East African coast in about the 10th century, and may have reached the US via trade routes eastward.

Vegetable travelers

Crops spread outward from their centers of diversity, first reaching the areas that were easily accessible by land or by short sea trips. Peas, for example, which originated in Asia, were found in Northern Europe in prehistoric times: archeologists have discovered seeds in excavations of Swiss Lake dwellings dating back to the Bronze Age, and two early Iron Age storage pits full of peas have been found in Southeast England. Broad beans were among the first crops to travel to Northern Europe, where prehistoric people would probably also have eaten a type of leafy non-heading cabbage, since wild cabbage is native to the coastal areas of Western Europe.

The beet family is another crop with European origins, and wild sea beets on the Mediterranean and Atlantic coasts were domesticated very long ago. At first developed for their green and red leaves, they gave rise to the spinach beets and chards that we know today. It was only in Roman times that more palatable cabbages, and other staple vegetables such as parsnips, onions, and carrots arrived in Western Europe. A few more exotic crops such as melons and cucumber were also introduced during this period, and others came with the Arabs and Jews a few centuries later.

Separated from Europe by the ocean, the development of vegetables in the Americas was entirely independent. Squash, corn (maize), and beans (runner, French, and lima beans) were cultivated in South America in ancient times. These important crops are referred to as the Three Sisters of traditional American agriculture. Intermixed, they protected and upheld each other as they grew: the beans provided nitrogen for growth; the corn stems provided supports for the beans to climb; and the long sprawling vines and large leaves of the squashes kept the soil beneath cool and moist for the other two Sisters. When the crops were

LEFT: *This attractive heirloom chard, known as Ruby or Rhubarb chard, is descended from a deep red variety which was once admired by Aristotle. Many early varieties of vegetable exhibited more intense colors than those commonly in cultivation today.*

harvested, they provided a diet balanced in car‐
bohydrates and vegetable protein.

There are records of the cultivation of
tomatoes and peppers growing in Central and
South America as early as the 5th century BC;
vivid portrayals of potatoes on early ceramics
found in Peru suggest that the vegetable had an
almost god-like status.

Europe and America originally had very
few crops in common, and the year 1492, when
Columbus first sailed to America, was a critical
one. After that date, the range of vegetable
crops on both continents increased enormously.
Along with gold and other Inca treasures, the
Spanish invaders of South America took
potatoes, tomatoes, beans, squashes, and peppers
back to Europe.

These vegetable curiosities were not always
readily accepted: runner beans, for example,
were first grown purely for their scarlet flowers,
and their edible qualities dismissed. Potatoes
suffered through the Europeans' ignorance, as
few were aware of the poisonous qualities of
the foliage, nor that, to be safe, tubers for eating
must be kept in the dark. Initially, therefore,
some people fell ill and died, which did not
enhance the potato's reception!

ITALIAN VEGETABLES

*Italy is in the Mediterranean
center of diversity. Although
few vegetable species actually
originated in this area, it is
an important secondary area
where numerous crops were
developed and improved.
Headed cabbages such as
Milan cabbage, and sweet or
Florence fennel (see above) are
obvious examples. Many beets,
chicories, lettuces, kales and
cauliflowers also came out
of Italy, and broccoli was
developed there as late as the
17th century.*

*Romanesco broccoli (see left)
is a recently revived heirloom
variety from Northern Italy,
where the head consists of
spiraling pale green florets
resembling a minaret.*

BEETS

A great diversity of beet varieties exist, from the two-tone concentric red and white rings of Dolce di Chiogga, through many rich purple varieties, to the golden skin and creamy yellow flesh of Golden Beet. The popularity of beet as a vegetable has suffered from its reputation as animal fodder, but many varieties have very delicate flavor, and they can also be very decorative.

LEFT: *Chinese cabbage is hardy and easy to grow, providing valuable greens at times of the year when there are few other leafy vegetables available.*

Traveling the other way across the Atlantic, the early settlers of North America took with them seeds of numerous crops unavailable in the New World. Surprisingly, although the homelands of the potato were relatively close at hand in Central and South America, this crop too was first introduced to North America via Europe.

Much of America's more recent vegetable heritage reflects the history of the many different immigrant groups that have come there. The past 150 years have seen huge migrations of population, and the US now treasures a rich patchwork of family heirlooms from northern countries such as Russia and Sweden, down through Germany and the rest of Central Europe, to those coming from as far south as Italy. Ironically, these heirlooms have sometimes been more diligently maintained by immigrant communities than in their countries of origin.

Although we are long past the time when newly discovered continents reveal completely new staple crops, some vegetables have moved across the world in relatively recent times. Chinese cabbage, for example, which was recorded in China as early as the 5th century AD, did not reach America and Europe until the end of the 19th century – probably brought from the East by missionaries. The value of many Oriental vegetables has only been recognized by Western gardeners in the last 10 or 20 years. Well adapted to cool temperate climates, these leafy vegetables make excellent fall and early spring crops, and tasty winter salad greens when little else is readily available.

Unlike the tropical latitudes of the developing world, which contain a rich indigenous diversity of nearly all the major vegetables, the Northern developed countries have always been reliant on travelers. Like our ancestors, we should continue to explore the potential of plants from other parts of the world which could increase the diversity of our food crops, as well as adding to our medicinal knowledge, and enrich our vegetable heritage.

How crops developed

Wherever in the world they originated, all our crops initially developed from wild plants. Primitive people were hunter-gatherers, killing wild animals and fish, and collecting leaves, nuts, roots, and berries for food. However, once groups started settling down in one place, they began to sow and tend some of the wild food plants and the domestication of crops began.

These early farmers knew nothing about genetics, but while working with their crops they would have spotted some plants that were better than others: those that grew more vigorously, or had larger and sweeter fruit, or thicker and more tender roots, for example. They would select these for saving seed, and the yields and qualities of the crop would gradually evolve, each generation improving upon the last. In the same way, undesirable characteristics such as prickles or bitterness were selected out. The farmers were in fact choosing plants with a more useful genetic make-up.

Sometimes natural crossing would occur between food crops and their wild relatives that were growing in the same field or in the field margins, producing plants that were quite different. Sudden spontaneous internal changes would also occasionally occur within plant cells, giving useful mutations, or 'sports', of the plant. By selecting these natural hybrids and sports for seed saving, new variations were developed.

For most of our crops, this process of domestication has been continuing for hundreds, sometimes thousands, of years, and they are far removed from their wild forms. Only a few crops, such as seakale (*Crambe maritima*) and corn salad (*Valerianella locusta*), are still easily recognizable in their natural state. A plump Savoy cabbage, or a cauliflower with tight white curds, bear little resemblance to their ancestral wild cabbage, a straggly unattractive creature. However, if you let some cultivated brassicas run to flower, they will reveal how similar they are to each other, and to the wild plants.

CULTIVATED CABBAGE

The earliest brassicas, which were descended directly from the wild cabbage, were rather unattractive plants, with tough glaucous leaves running up a thick straggling stem.

Over centuries, the species developed to produce many varieties beautiful enough to grace any ornamental landscape, such as the finely veined and curled leaves of this Savoy cabbage in frost.

KALES

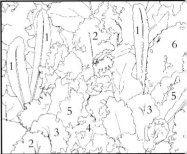

1. Lacinato

2. Russian Red

3. Halbhoher Moosbacher
   Winter Hellgrüner

4. Siberian

5. Krasnaya Kuroavafa
   Vysokaja

6. Niedriger Grüner
   Feinstekrause

THE DIVERSITY OF TOMATOES

Some tomatoes – such as Red Currant, or Broad Ripple Yellow Currant (*see right*) – have fruits that are little more than the size of blackcurrants. They are best harvested by shaking the plant upside down. In contrast, the old beefsteak variety Big Rainbow can have fruit weighing 3lb or more.

The color of a tomato depends on both its skin membrane color and the color of the flesh. A red-fleshed tomato with a translucent skin looks pink, and a tomato with a yellow flesh and translucent skin looks pale yellow. Some white tomatoes do have flesh that is also almost white. At the opposite color extreme are

the 'black' tomatoes, many of which were developed in Russia: Black Krim from the Black Sea, for example, has very dark brownish purple skin and reddish-brown flesh.

Yellow Pear, which dates from the late 1800s, is (as its name suggests) pear-shaped; others are bulbous and deeply ribbed such as the Mexican variety Zapotec (*see below*), believed to be the ancestor of all beefsteak-type tomatoes.

Their internal structure also varies – paste or processing tomatoes have a solid flesh, often described as meaty, with few seeds. Stuffing tomatoes are almost hollow inside, the seeds

are clustered together in the center and can be easily removed, making the fruit ideal for filling with savory mixtures. One interesting lobed type, known by Central American Indians as a 'traveler tomato', consists of many individual cavities so that the fruit can be divided simply by tearing it apart – no picnic knife needed!

The most important characteristic of the tomato for gardeners is, of course, taste. The gel around the seeds significantly affects the flavor of the fruit, particularly its acidity, and how it feels in the mouth. The less acid the gel of a particular variety, the sweeter the fruit – although growing conditions also play a part, and most varieties are sweeter if grown in plenty of sunshine. Paste tomatoes with few seeds (and therefore little gel) are rather bland, without the taste or texture desirable in a salad tomato.

Adaptation to climate

As crops that are domesticated in one area move to a neighboring area, where perhaps rainfall is higher, or frost more severe, or the soil heavier, they gradually adapt to the new conditions. In each generation, some plants survive the particular conditions better than others, and these – aided by farmer selection – contribute disproportionately more to the next generation. Differences in conditions between neighboring areas are often subtle ones, but occasionally plants have had to adapt to more marked changes – as when crops used to the tropical conditions of South America were first brought to Europe, with its shorter growing seasons and longer days.

People in different regions may have different tastes and needs – preferring potatoes with denser tubers, for example, or with purple skins – and this has always influenced the way a crop has developed. A wide range of local crop types known as 'landraces' traditionally evolved in response to such different situations, each with distinct traits, but lacking the uniformity of today's highly bred vegetable varieties. Landraces are sometimes referred to as 'folk varieties', recognizing the important role that rural communities have played (and still play) in developing and maintaining them.

As crops become adapted to climate and soil conditions, they also develop defenses against local pests and diseases. When a pest or disease overcomes a particular defense mechanism within the plant, that crop will readapt, and so will the pest, and so on. Plants and their predators have always evolved alongside each other. Wide-ranging pest and disease resistance is an important feature of the old landraces.

THE POTATO IN EUROPE

The potato that came to Europe from South America in the late 16th century did not produce the abundance of smooth round tubers that we expect to harvest from our plants today. The tubers were small and knobbly, the plants were susceptible to infection, and yields were low.

It was grown initially as a garden curiosity rather than a serious crop – in England in 1716 it was considered much less important than the radish. This poor performance was not solely because of the change of climate, but because the life cycle of these potatoes was dependent on the short equatorial days in their homeland.

Gradually the crop began to adapt to longer growing days – and by the mid 18th century was widely grown on a commercial basis, both for human and animal consumption. Even in the Nordic countries, further still removed from the potatoes' tropical origins, varieties were developed which did well in the very long days and cool short growing seasons. Some of the old Nordic varieties still in existence today are particularly valued for their long dormancy times and resistance to certain storage diseases.

SWEET PEPPERS

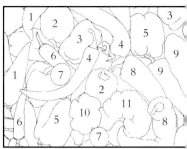

1. Pimiento

2. Lorelei

3. Gold Star

4. Jimmy Nardello's

5. Ariane

6. Tequila Sunrise

7. Sweet Cherry

8. Early Prolific Banana

9. Sweet Melrose

10. Red Cheese Pimento

11. Quadrati D'Asti Giallo

Modern plant breeding

For millennia, farmers and gardeners were the plant breeders, improving crops by selection from generation to generation. In the 19th century, rather than waiting for changes to occur at random in nature, a few experimenters started to make deliberate crosses between plants. By choosing the plants carefully, these early hybridizers hoped that the offspring would have the desirable characteristics of both parents.

The Vilmorin-Andrieux family in France were pioneers in European plant breeding in the 19th century, as was Luther Burbank in the United States, gaining particular fame for his work with potatoes. However, it was only when the experimental work of the Austro-Silesian monk Gregor Mendel was recognized in the early 1900s that hybridization gained a real scientific basis, and gave more predictable results. Prior to that, it had been largely a hit and miss affair.

At first new varieties were developed by individuals and small family-based seedsmen, still with the involvement of farmers and gardeners, but techniques gradually became more sophisticated. There were also pressures to make plants of the same variety less variable, so those with slightly 'wrong' characteristics (for commercial purposes) were weeded out. Over several generations varieties were developed that were very uniform and reproduced that uniformity; these were known as 'pure lines'. In the 1930s the first 'F1 hybrid' corn varieties were produced, the seed coming from crossing two inbred pure lines. F1 hybrids of other crops soon followed.

In the last 25 years, plant breeding has become the specialist realm of microbiologists, geneticists and other scientists. It is a complex major industry. Dozens of potato varieties, for

LONG-KEEPING TOMATOES

A tomato that would stay fresh and firm on the supermarket shelf for weeks was the marketing dream that inspired the variety Flavr Savr. Genetic engineers spliced in genes to change the enzyme polygalacturonase, which naturally occurs in the fruits, so that they would decompose more slowly. As a result, it was said that the Flavr Savr tomato would stay in good condition for up to 50 days.

Yet many traditional tomato varieties already have very long shelf life. Before tomatoes could be imported out of season, they were deliberately selected so that they could be stored for several months and used in the winter. Garden Peach, for example, is an heirloom variety with excellent keeping qualities. Orange-pink fruit ripens very slowly off the vine, and stores well without loss of taste or texture. Traditional gardeners used to pick these in fall, and would still be eating them after Christmas.

example, can be screened for blight resistance in the glasshouse within 3-4 weeks of germination, rather than growing them in a field for several months, and any useful material resulting can be held in test tubes using tissue culture. Genetic engineering allows specific genes in plants to be located and marked in the laboratory, and then moved between species in a way that was never possible with traditional hybridization methods.

Today farmers and gardeners are seldom involved in plant development. It is geared to the perceived needs of industry, which is typically concerned with relatively short-term gain. Plant breeding has also become extremely expensive: for example, the development and marketing of one of the first genetically engineered varieties to be released, the Flavr Savr tomato (*see facing page*), is said to have cost in excess of 95 million US dollars. With such investment, it is no wonder that a few varieties dominate the shelves of superstores, and the pages of catalogs.

THE EARLY DAYS

We have come a long way since the days when the Mayflower sailed from Plymouth in 1620, taking the Pilgrim Fathers to establish the first English colony in North America. Ever since then, seeds have been carried by migrants round the world. A ship sailing from England to North America in 1631 carried supplies of parsnip, beet, cabbage, carrot, cauliflower, leek, onion and radish seed, none of which would have then been obtainable across the Atlantic. The most expensive item then was two ounces of cauliflower seeds which cost five shillings or 35 cents.

F1 HYBRIDS AND OPEN-POLLINATED VARIETIES

The creation of an F1 hybrid first involves selecting two parent plants with desired characteristics and inbreeding them (not allowing them to exchange pollen with others) until two very pure, distinct, and uniform lines are produced. These lines are then married, all the pollen coming from one parent and all the egg cells from the other. The resulting seed is what you buy in an expensive packet of an F1 hybrid variety. It will give you progeny (the F1 or first filial generation) which all have the desirable traits from both parents, and which all exhibit 'hybrid vigor'. This means that they will usually outgrow and outyield plants of traditional open-pollinated varieties.

Unfortunately, the seeds of these F1 plants do not produce the same high class offspring, but a motley selection – and sometimes the seeds will not germinate at all. In contrast, the seeds of open-pollinated varieties will produce offspring that are true-to-type, although without the same strict uniformity as F1 hybrids.

❷
THE IMPORTANCE OF DIVERSITY

ABOVE: *Traditional in Italy, this majestic onion came to the US via David Cavagnaro's family.*

LEFT: *Kohl rabi, scorzonera, and salsify are as easy to grow as the commoner roots such as parsnips, rutabaga, beets, and carrots.*

Now that vigorous F1 hybrids dominate the seed catalogues, and crops can be tailored to our needs by genetic engineering, it is tempting to think that the old varieties are redundant. It is true that new varieties do give high yields under the right conditions; they can have good resistance to specific pests and diseases; they make harvest times predictable, and they have made enormous and valuable contributions to the world's food-producing capacity. The danger is that they will cause us to abandon and neglect the broad genetic base of our traditional wild and cultivated plants.

Modern plant breeding on its own can never provide solutions to every question, and traditional open-pollinated varieties, landraces or folk varieties, and their wild relatives will always have crucial roles to play. They have indispensable qualities and a diversity in their genetic make-up which cannot be replaced.

It was lack of such diversity early in plant-breeding history that led to the Irish potato famine of 1845. After the potato was introduced into Europe from South America in the 16th century, it took time to adapt to northern conditions, but by the 1840s it was widely grown, and had become a staple food in Ireland. In the autumn of 1845, the potatoes there were struck by a devastating and previously unknown fungal disease – so virulent that some correspondents at the time labeled it 'cholera', but we now identify it as late blight. Any gardener who has experienced this disease will know just how quickly it can spread through potato foliage, and will recognize the unmistakable stench it creates as the tubers rot.

One million people died in Ireland in 1846; another million emigrated. In many areas farmers lost 90% of their tubers and it took a decade for the situation to recover. This epidemic happened because all the varieties of potato growing in Europe at that time were derived from just two parent varieties, the two brought from the Andes that had adapted most successfully to the northern climate. They produced reliable yields in the cool wet conditions of Northern Europe, but Andean potatoes had never encountered blight and so had no resistance to it. Once the disease got a hold on one plant, there was nothing to stop it spreading quickly to attack all the rest.

Such epidemics of monoculture have happened since, destroying crops of wheat, corn, and rice in different areas of the world (*see pages 41 and 48*).

Past, present, and future

In the 1850s, after the potato famine years, growers in Europe realized the importance of using a wider spread of parent varieties for breeding. They imported more varieties from America for developing the crop, and widened its genetic characteristics. However, it was not until the 20th century, when scientific expeditions collected wild potatoes from Central and South America, that European varieties with significant resistance to blight began to be developed. In the 1950s and early 1960s, several potatoes containing resistance genes from the Mexican species *Solanum demissum* were bred in the UK. High resistance to blight has also recently been found in other Mexican species such as *Solanum papita* and *Solanum polydenum*.

Scientists working on the development of other major crops are also using landraces and wild ancestors of vegetables from the centers of diversity. Until very recently, most commercially grown varieties of soya beans in the US were derived from a handful of imported lines; their narrow genetic base made them vulnerable to epidemics. Now seed from 500 different soya bean strains has been brought to the US from Central China, where the bean originated, and these are being used in current breeding programs. One of the problems they may help to solve is that of *phytophthora* root rot – a major fungal disease of soya beans, which can kill seedlings and reduce yields of older plants, particularly on poorly drained soils. Not surprisingly, resistance to this disease has been found predominantly in soya bean lines from rainy wet areas of Central China.

Similarly, wild lettuces such as *Lactuca serriola* are being used to breed resistance against downy mildew into modern iceberg lettuce (*see page* 45), and hybridization of the cultivated tomato *Lycopersicon esculentum* with wild species such as *L. pimpinellifolium* has been used to confer pest and disease resistance on many of the new varieties on the market today.

Traditional varieties, selected by farmers and gardeners over many years and generations of cultivation, are more closely related to modern ones, but these old varieties can also be important to plant breeders. Developed because of their reliability and adaptability, they are more likely to thrive without chemical fertilizers, pesticides, or irrigation than their modern counterparts. Some of them will also have good storage qualities dating back to the days before refrigeration and controlled atmosphere storage. These are just the sort of characteristics that could be valuable in years to come.

No one really knows what the future holds, no matter how many predictions scientists come up with. Global warming may give many places more extreme conditions – hotter summers, harder frosts, extended droughts. Less ozone in the atmosphere is already causing an increase in ultra-violet rays, and who knows what pests and diseases might arise in 10, 50, or 100 years time? We can only guess at the long-term effects on plants. Modern plant breeders may be able to create new varieties with some of the required traits, but they can only do so by making use of existing ones – they cannot create new genes.

Many characteristics of our wild crops and old varieties are as yet unnoticed, unvalued, unrecognized, or unneeded. These qualities may be vitally important in the future. By preserving as diverse a range of plants as possible, we will have the greatest chance of adapting future varieties as the situation demands. Otherwise we are putting the security of all our future food supplies in jeopardy.

Recycled genes

Through scientific and technological advances we now know how to use wild crop species and old landraces in plant breeding, but this rarely offers successful simple solutions.

You only have to look at the difference between a tall spindly wild lettuce and a large-hearted iceberg to see the difficulties involved in using the wild form as a parent. Similarly, wild tomatoes may have extremely desirable qualities of disease resistance, but they also have many less attractive characteristics such as tiny fruits, and rampant growth. Breeding the good qualities into a modern crop, whilst eliminating the undesirable ones, takes long and expensive breeding programs.

Plant breeders are much more likely to get reliable results quickly, and cheaply, if they work from closely related plants. So commercial pressures to save time and money mean that many modern varieties are simply remixtures of each other. There is little true variation in their genetic make-up, and within each variety the plants are extremely uniform. This means that even when some new genetic material has been introduced into a crop, the beneficial results may be limited.

If disease resistance is conferred on a variety by one major gene, and this variety or a similar one is planted over a large area, the resistance will soon break down. The greater the contin-uous area of similar varieties that the disease encounters, the greater will be the pressure on it to adapt and spread. This is what happened to the first blight-resistant potatoes that were developed containing a simple type of resistance using genes from the wild species *Solanum demissum*. The fungus soon adapted and evolved strains which made this type of blight resistance almost useless.

A disastrous outbreak of the fungal disease Southern leaf blight in America's corn crop in 1970 illustrates the problem caused by plant breeders 'recycling' genes. Since the 1950s, most corn grown commercially in the US had consisted of hybrid varieties bred using material from one male sterile variety, giving plants tassels with impotent pollen. This prevented self-pollination and made the process of hybridization much easier and cheaper. Up till then the tassels had had to be removed by hand.

Unfortunately this same common feature made all the varieties susceptible to leaf blight. In the summer of 1970, this disease ruined the corn crop. In the Southern States many farmers lost their entire crop, and in the US as a whole, 15% of the crop was lost.

Despite this warning, nearly all commercial corn – both that for grinding into cornmeal or flour and that for sweetcorn – now consists of just a few genetically similar hybrid varieties. Compare this to the two or three hundred local landraces of corn that the American Indians were growing when the first Europeans arrived – corns with amazingly wide genetic diversity. They varied in the color and form of the grain, and were tailored to the local environment, and their end use (*see page 56*). They were tended on numerous small plots – a far cry from the monocultures found today. The first European settlers adopted these various local varieties, and it was not until the mid 1800s that the emphasis changed to value larger, more uniform ears, and much of the diversity was lost. Then in the 1930s the first hybrid corns were produced.

Some primitive corns are still available through specialist seed suppliers in the US concerned with protecting and maintaining endangered plants, and a few traditional farmers also still maintain commercial varieties of open-pollinated corn.

POTATOES

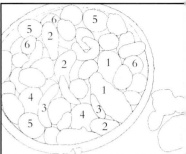

1. Siberian
2. Purple Peruvian
3. German Finger
4. Ashworth
5. Red Erik
6. Caribe

Protection through diversity

One of the best ways to combat the effects of a pest or disease outbreak is to plant mixed crops, using traditional varieties with more variable characteristics. Even where a disease may find it easy to overcome one plant, it will probably struggle to make inroads to the next few. Their leaf surfaces might be less easily penetrated, for example, or the fungus might not be able to spread quickly through their tissues. Usually a combination of factors is responsible for the resistance, and because some plants are vulnerable, there is not the same pressure on the disease to overcome it. Even though the overall yield of such a mixed crop will never be as high as that of a single immune variety, it will never run the risk of being devastated by an epidemic.

It is difficult to get such lasting resistance in a single modern variety. It usually means working with many different genes and is a considerable challenge to the plant breeder. Even then other unexpected problems may occur. Just as plants of uniform modern varieties can have the same susceptibility to an unexpected pest or disease, so will they all have the same reaction to any other kind of environmental change. Only by maintaining a wide genetic base will plants have the chance to survive in the future.

Traditional methods of gardening and farming are not only important because they maintain old varieties as an essential raw material for plant breeding, they also encapsulate a whole world of valuable information about selection, propagation, seed saving, cultivation, and use of the crop. The traditional ways of growing crops often illustrate the best ways of protecting diversity. This knowledge must not be allowed to die out.

RESPONSES TO DISEASE

Late blight, the fungus behind the Irish potato famine, originates in Mexico, where most varieties have therefore developed some type of resistance. However, the disease evolves to try and overcome resistance, so every year some strain of blight attacks Mexican potato crops.

To minimize the effect of these attacks, Mexican farmers plant up to 30 varieties in a single field. They cannot predict where the blight will strike, and recognize that some variety, or varieties, will inevitably succumb. But the others will survive and flourish, so the farmers will always have a potato harvest even if parts of the crop fail. Their entire crop will never be devastated.

The response in more 'developed' agricultural systems is different. A few varieties are planted over large areas, so the blight fungus quickly overcomes any inbred resistance that they have. To prevent epidemics, the potato growers must therefore spray their crops routinely with fungicides. The plant breeders breed new 'resistant' varieties, but the high cost of the breeding programs dictates that they must sell a few varieties widely to recoup the cost – so these few varieties are planted over a large area... and the problem carries on.

LUMPERS POTATO

A late maincrop variety giving excellent yields of large knobbly tubers, Lumpers was the mainstay of Irish potato plantings at the time of the 1845 famine. It was highly susceptible if blight struck in July before the tubers had bulked up.

Outside Ireland the variety was said to have poor flavor and little culinary merit. But when museum stocks were grown out in 1995, marking the 150th anniversary of the famine, many people remarked how good it was to eat – probably compared to most varieties commercially grown today.

LETTUCE BREEDING FOR DOWNY MILDEW RESISTANCE

A high proportion of all fungicide applications to commercial varieties of lettuce in Northern Europe are administered in the attempt to control downy mildew. This disease has developed races which have overcome nearly all current resistance in commercial lettuce varieties. Breeding for mildew resistance is an important part of a 20 year lettuce breeding program in the UK at the Horticultural Research International (HRI). Scientists there are using four wild lettuce varieties *Lactuca serriola*, *L. virosa*, *L. aculeata* and *L. salinga* as sources of new resistance genes.

The biggest problem in the program has been to obtain a lettuce that has both resistance and acceptable quality, as wild lettuce are far removed from consumers' ideas of what constitutes an acceptable lettuce. Whereas the marketplace wants crisp-leaved and tight-hearted lettuces, wild varieties tend to be long stemmed and straggly, with uneven leaf growth. It has taken two decades to produce iceberg varieties containing one of the new resistant genes, now being trialed by commercial growers.

These varieties are successful at present, but it is only a matter of time before new races of downy mildew will evolve to overcome their resistance. So scientists are also looking at ways of using the old variety Iceberg, or Batavia Blonde. This lettuce has good resistance to downy mildew, resistance that seems to have lasted since at least the middle of the last century without threat from evolved races of the disease.

Still grown by gardeners today, Batavia Blonde appeared in a seed list from the Vilmorin seed company in 1856. Although it is not actually immune to downy mildew, the disease does not spread through a whole crop in the way that it affects other varieties – fewer plants are infected, and the symptoms of the infected plants are less severe.

The reason that this old lettuce variety is not attacked in the same way as others is due to the complex genetics of the resistance – probably involving at least six genes. This makes the effect much stronger than if it were conferred by one single gene; however it also makes the resistance much more difficult for scientists to isolate.

LETTUCES

LEFT: Reine des Glaces is a tight headed gourmet lettuce from France. Its lace-fringed leaves are deeply cut, and pointed, adding a special touch to any salad.

BELOW (TOP): The light yellow-green leaves of Australian Yellow are very tender and slightly sweet; this variety is excellent for hot climates as it does not bolt easily.

BELOW (BOTTOM): Although Bronze Arrow is a California heirloom, it is hardy and adaptable, suitable for most climates. The large leaves are shaped like arrowheads, green with a reddish bronze tinge.

High yielding varieties

The overriding factor which determines whether a new variety is judged successful is yield. Even when plant breeders are looking for other characteristics such as disease resistance, only varieties whose yields are at least as good as their rivals are likely to be considered for development. However, yield is typically measured on monitored test sites with high inputs of chemical fertilizers and pesticides, and with optimum irrigation.

Modern varieties perform well in such 'ideal' conditions, but can fail dramatically when they are less favorable. This has had particularly disastrous results for farmers in developing countries swept up in the so-called 'Green Revolution'. In the late 1960s high-yield varieties of wheat and rice were developed, mainly in American and Japanese breeding programs. These new varieties responded well to applications of nitrogen fertilizer, and initially had some resistance to major pests and diseases. They were soon replacing traditional varieties used by peasant farmers, who were promised reliable plants with amazingly high yields, despite poor conditions.

At first initial production was greatly increased. However, the pests and diseases quickly adapted, and the new strains began to need not only fertilizers, but pesticides and fungicides. They also needed herbicides, because the high levels of fertilizer promoted weed growth, and machinery to apply these sprays. Irrigation schemes were also essential. Seeds of the new strains were in many cases initially too expensive for subsistence farmers to purchase, and they became dependent on additional costly inputs – without them, the new varieties were often less productive than the old ones. One of the causes of the Ethiopian famine in the 1980s was the fact that the country had abandoned its traditional drought-tolerant crops and varieties for new ones.

Around the same time, another problem with high-yield varieties occurred in the Philippines, when a 'miracle' hybrid strain of rice was hit by disease, destroying whole crops. Rice growers switched to another hybrid form, which proved vulnerable to other diseases and pests; so farmers moved on to yet another hybrid that was resistant to almost all local diseases and pests, but vulnerable to wind. When breeders eventually decided to return to a traditional strain that had grown well in harsh weather, they found this strain was now almost unavailable as indigenous farmers had planted all their rice fields with the 'miracle' hybrids.

Yet another disadvantage of the new varieties has been their failure to fit in with local farming systems. For example, hybrid varieties of wheat had short stems which did not provide straw for feeding animals or thatching roofs. Moreover, many of the farmers who for centuries had saved seed of their traditional varieties for the next year's crop found that this was no longer possible. Either the varieties were hybrids, so saved seed failed to give a good crop in the second and subsequent years, or their disease resistance had broken down to the point where they needed to be replaced with the latest (temporarily) less susceptible strains.

Although the consequences are, in the short term, nowhere near so far-reaching, the same problem applies to modern vegetable varieties grown by gardeners and small organic growers, particularly on marginal land or in difficult climates. The conditions under which new varieties are developed are often very different to those in your backyard, and traditional varieties – particularly those of local origin – will probably outperform the new ones.

Gardeners' needs

Traditional varieties have other qualities that make them more useful to gardeners and small growers than their modern counterparts. Modern varieties of many vegetables, such as peas and corn, are bred to mature all at once so that they can be harvested by machine, and new brassica and lettuce varieties will all head simultaneously to satisfy the commercial market. Home gardeners do not want such gluts and famines. Beware of catalog descriptions that say a variety is 'good for freezing' – this usually means that it will need harvesting all at once. Traditional varieties – tall peas, old types of lettuce, open-pollinated sweetcorn, cabbage, and cauliflower – are more likely to crop over a long period.

Processors and supermarkets want uniform crops – carrots the same length, parsnips the same shape, cauliflowers the same size – so that they can be packed and priced by machine. They are also looking for resistance to bruising, so that vegetables are not damaged by being sorted on a conveyor belt, or by traveling long distances from the grower to a centralized packing house and back out again. It has been said that new hybrid tomatoes destined for the US supermarket trade are tested in the same Florida laboratory that tests car fenders!

Gardeners, however, like to harvest according to the recipe and the occasion, and variation in the size of vegetables can be a positive advantage. Produce only has to survive a trip up the garden path; far from wanting tomatoes with tough skins, they want fruit that dissolves in the mouth or on cooking, as many traditional varieties do.

What gardeners want above all is taste, yet this seems rarely considered as a priority in modern vegetable breeding programs. It is a quality that is mentioned again and again in descriptions of old varieties, whether they are leafy crops, roots, or fruits. Of course, even a standard hybrid variety does taste better grown at home and gathered fresh rather than picked from a supermarket, but the sweet perfumed taste of, for example, some of the heirloom melons, such as the 19th century French Noir des Carmes, or the British Blenheim Orange is unsurpassed. The cantaloupe variety Old Time Tennessee is said to be so fragrant that you can find the melons in the dark!

OPEN-POLLINATED SWEETCORN

Most sweetcorn varieties sold to gardeners are now F1 hybrids. Their cobs are uniform in size, and tend to mature all at once, only an advantage if you want to freeze them. The newest hybrid corns contain special genes to make them 'supersweet', they are very sugary and hold their sweetness for some time after they have been picked – a useful attribute for supermarket sales, but quite unnecessary for home gardeners. Moreover, these varieties can be difficult to germinate in less than ideal conditions, and the seedlings often lack vigor.

Many gardeners still prefer the taste of the traditional open-pollinated sweetcorns such as Golden Bantam. This was introduced by Burpee in 1902 and until recently was widely available both in the US and Europe. However, even this old favorite variety has recently been dropped from the lists of all the major commercial companies.

RAINBOW CHARD

Some strikingly attractive
varieties, now fashionable
for their decorative qualities
in modern potagers and
edible landscapes, are in fact
of very ancient origin.

A red chard, ancestor of
the widely grown Rhubarb
or Ruby chard, which has
bright red leaf stalks, was
described by Aristotle in
the 4th century. In 1885, in
The Vegetable Garden,
Vilmorin listed Chilian
Beet or Red-stalked Swiss
Chard grown as an orna-
mental plant and for a table
vegetable. The book also
mentions a yellow form.

This Rainbow chard is a
spectacular mixture of the
vivid colors which have
been found in old varieties.

Links with the past

Traditional varieties are not only of practical value for present and future gardeners, they also provide inextricable links to local history and local culture; to major historical events, and to other people in other times.

The potato, Lumpers, for example, provides a direct historical link to the Irish potato famine, illustrating the potential disasters inherent in lack of diversity. Other varieties have purely local relevance. Particular agriculture practices have historically affected the pattern of work and the nature of the landscape. Local businesses such as that of the French 'Onion Johnnies' selling Brittany's Roscoff onions, developed on the strength of certain crops (*see page 57*). Local festivals and customs associated with particular varieties have grown up all over the world, such as the tradition, in North East England, of eating Carlin peas on 'Carlin Sunday' (*see right*).

Religious significance has sometimes become attached to certain varieties. Many of the diverse colored corns of Native American tribes were used for sacred rituals, and spiritual significance has also been attributed to the fascinatingly beautiful markings and forms of bean seeds. The large number of old landraces of drying peas in Sweden is said to be due to their pre-Christian tradition of eating pea soup on Thursdays – the Swedish people were said to believe that peas were the food of their god Thor, and Thursday was 'Thor's day'.

To immigrant families in any country, seeds brought from their homelands were not only important to maintain their diet but to keep alive a link with their roots, even more so when emigration had been by necessity rather than choice. The Cherokee Indians Trail of Tears bean (*see opposite page*) came to symbolize their struggle against hard times.

CARLIN PEAS

Carlin peas are drying peas dating back to 16th century England, still traditionally eaten in the North East of the country on 'Carlin Sunday', the fifth Sunday in Lent, two weeks before Easter.

The tradition is said to commemorate the relief of the famine that occurred in the area when it was besieged in 1644. Famine ended when a shipwreck threw up a cargo of Carlin peas, retrieved by the hungry people.

Carlins are small black peas with a slight mottle. The night before Carlin Sunday they are steeped in water, and the next day they are boiled, often with a ham bone or bacon fat, until they are soft and mushy.

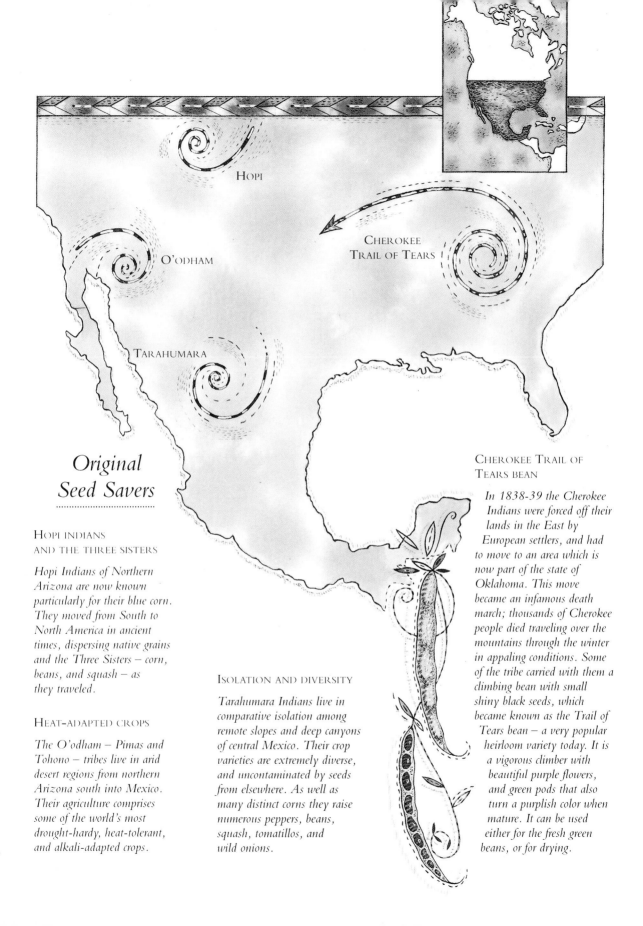

HOPI

O'ODHAM

CHEROKEE
TRAIL OF TEARS

TARAHUMARA

Original Seed Savers

HOPI INDIANS AND THE THREE SISTERS

Hopi Indians of Northern Arizona are now known particularly for their blue corn. They moved from South to North America in ancient times, dispersing native grains and the Three Sisters – corn, beans, and squash – as they traveled.

HEAT-ADAPTED CROPS

The O'odham – Pimas and Tohono – tribes live in arid desert regions from northern Arizona south into Mexico. Their agriculture comprises some of the world's most drought-hardy, heat-tolerant, and alkali-adapted crops.

ISOLATION AND DIVERSITY

Tarahumara Indians live in comparative isolation among remote slopes and deep canyons of central Mexico. Their crop varieties are extremely diverse, and uncontaminated by seeds from elsewhere. As well as many distinct corns they raise numerous peppers, beans, squash, tomatillos, and wild onions.

CHEROKEE TRAIL OF TEARS BEAN

In 1838-39 the Cherokee Indians were forced off their lands in the East by European settlers, and had to move to an area which is now part of the state of Oklahoma. This move became an infamous death march; thousands of Cherokee people died traveling over the mountains through the winter in appaling conditions. Some of the tribe carried with them a climbing bean with small shiny black seeds, which became known as the Trail of Tears bean – a very popular heirloom variety today. It is a vigorous climber with beautiful purple flowers, and green pods that also turn a purplish color when mature. It can be used either for the fresh green beans, or for drying.

CORNS

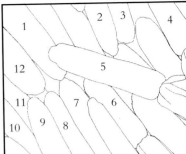

1. Reid's Yellow

2. Rainbow Dent

3. Mandan Red Flour

4. Strubbe's Calico

5. Northwest Red Dent

6. Strubbe's Purple

7. Northern Bloody Butcher

8. Hickory King

9. Blue Clarage

10. Purple Husk Cob

11. Narragousett

12. Southern Bloody Butcher

NATIVE AMERICAN CORNS

The Native American word for corn 'mahiz', means 'our life'. Corn is their prime food of life, it is also vital in many sacred rituals. They traditionally culture six colors of corn: black, red, white, yellow, blue and multicolored. Each color represents one of the Six Directions – north, east, south, west, zenith (Father Sky) and nadir (Mother Earth). In different areas, different colors have become specialties, in response to growing conditions and particular preferences. For example Northeastern Indians use white corn for breads, while blue corn is the choice of the Southwestern Indians.

Atlantic Coast Indians provided the first settlers with corn, and taught them how to pound or grind it for bread. These early settlers went on to develop their own colors and varieties. Sweetcorn developed relatively recently, created by natural mutations from flint or dent corn around the mid 1700s.

Southwestern Indian corns have evolved in association with beneficial soil fungi, mycorrhizae, which make the roots 10 times more efficient in extracting soil nutrients. These fungi cease to function at high chemical fertilizer levels. Some of the old Native American corn fields are over 800 years old; they have never been fertilized, the fertility has been maintained by mycorrhizae and through inter-planting with beans.

PEAS BEFORE THE FREEZER

Peas for drying have been grown since ancient times, but peas used fresh from the pod did not become popular until the 16th century when new strains were developed by Italian gardeners. These first shelling peas had smooth round seeds and were very hardy. Their descendants are still used by gardeners today to make early and overwintering sowings, extending the harvest of fresh peas. One of the oldest round-seeded peas still in cultivation, Prince Albert, was probably introduced around 1840, the year Albert married Queen Victoria. Sown in January, it can produce a crop of peas in May, and if some of these are saved and sown in July, they will crop in September.

In the 18th century came a different strain of sweeter but less hardy peas, easily distinguished by their seeds which have a wrinkled appearance. The first varieties of these sweet podding peas were very tall, growing to 2m (6ft 6in) or more, and cropped over a long period.

When these varieties were first grown on a field scale, they had to be picked and podded by hand. In the early 1900s, children in pea-growing areas of England were allowed six weeks' holiday from school during the pea harvest so that they could help with picking, and the pods were shelled and graded by gangs of women at Covent Garden Market in London.

It was not until much later in the 20th century that modern dwarf peas were developed, tailored to mechanical harvesting and deep freezing. The plants of these varieties are often less than 3 feet tall with a deliberately shortened flowering period so that pods are nearly all ready at exactly the same time. Conveniently for the harvester, the peas are mostly borne at the top of the plants, and many of these varieties have few leaves.

These qualities are not generally useful to gardeners, and it is worth seeking out some of the tall garden pea varieties that are still in cultivation such as Ne Plus Ultra (introduced in 1847) and Champion of England (1843). These varieties crop over a long period and have good overall yields. They can also be very ornamental: when the tall pea Magnum Bonum with its beautiful white flowers was displayed at the Chelsea Flower Show in London in 1992, many people mistook it for a sweet pea. Some other tall peas have lemon yellow or dark purple pods; some varieties are delicious fresh, others are good for soups or drying.

Vegetable names and histories

The names of old vegetable varieties often link them with people, places, or history, and hint at a story to be told. In the US, vegetables are often connected with people – individuals or communities. Heirloom varieties such as Grandpa Admires lettuce, Bill Jump's soup pea, or Boothby's Blond cucumber indicate how varieties have been handed down though generations of one family. Many ancient varieties are named for their original breeders – Aztec Red Kidney, or Montezuma's Red beans – while the importance of Native American seed-savers is remembered in varieties such as Mandan Bride corn, or Hopi Black beans.

Many varieties came to the US with waves of immigrants, and you need only look at any page of a seed catalog to find names of seeds which reflect their country of origin – Irish Cobbler and Swedish Peanut Fingerling potatoes, Old German and Costuloto Genovese tomatoes, and hundreds of others.

In Northern Europe, the market garden regions which supplied vegetables to the expanding industrial cities of the 18th and 19th centuries were particularly significant in the development of vegetable varieties. These areas produced countless distinct local strains. The Vale of Evesham (serving industrial towns in the English Midlands) gave its name to numerous varieties such as the Evesham Special Brussels sprout, while market garden areas serving Paris produced hundreds of locally recorded varieties – De Viroflay spinach, Milan de Pontoise cabbage and the onion Paille des Vertus are still popular today.

Other names tie in with folklore, like the Turkey Craw bean, a productive climbing snap bean grown by some US seed savers, the original seed of which is said to have come from the craw of a turkey brought home by a hunter!

L'OIGNON DE ROSCOFF

Legend says that the pink Roscoff onion was brought to Brittany from Portugal by a local man from the town of Roscoff, who traveled along the western European coasts with Breton boats in the 16th century. The variety adapted well to the local weather and soil conditions in this corner of France, and flourished in a way that other onions have never done. It became very important to the local growers and the local diet.

In the mid 19th century, one farmer tried taking some onions across the Channel to sell in England and Wales – and such was his success that many others followed. By the end of the century there were 2000 of the French 'Onion Johnnies', traditionally dressed in blue and white striped jerseys and black berets, riding round the UK on bicycles festooned with onions. Up to the second World War, the Roscoff area still produced up to 50,000 tonnes of the special pink onions a year, each grower having his own strain and saving his own seed.

Roscoff onions are very mild and sweet, good in salads and salsas. They also store well. Although production is much less today, the variety is still grown commercially in Brittany, and there are still some Onion Johnnies traveling the UK – although times have changed, and most have exchanged their traditional bicycles for smart vans.

3

PRESSURES FOR UNIFORMITY

Despite the importance of traditional vegetable varieties, landraces and their wild ancestors, they are fast disappearing. Numerous interrelated factors are conspiring to force old varieties out and replace them with new ones. Pressures supporting this trend towards uniform modern varieties arise from the dominance of multinational companies in the seed trade, modern farming methods, industrial development with its related social pressures, and from the legislation governing the sales of seeds.

ABOVE: *Traditional varieties of peas, like these snow peas, usually grow at least six feet tall, with pods at all heights.*

LEFT: *Round-headed cabbage varieties such as the old European Dittmarshcer Früher store well without losing flavor.*

The statistics showing the extent of losses are frightening. In the US and Canada, two thirds of the nearly 5000 non-hybrid vegetable varieties that were offered in 1984 catalogs had been dropped by 1994. The situation is even worse in Europe, where substantial numbers of traditional varieties – often those adapted to local climates and cultures – which were available until two decades ago can no longer be obtained. For example, in France the 1925 seed list of the Vilmorin seed company offered more varieties of cabbages, beetroot, melons, and onions, than were available on the entire French seed market in the 1980s.

Gardeners do not need to read these figures to be convinced. Each year they find that yet more of their favorite varieties have disappeared from the seed catalogs, and have been replaced by new hybrids. Even where the traditional open-pollinated varieties are still offered on the market, their existence is fragile since many of them are available from just one supplier. In 1994, about 50% of all open-pollinated vegetable varieties (in the UK, the US and Canada) were such 'one source' varieties. If such a supply dries up, the variety is gone for ever.

For some vegetable species, the influx of new varieties has had particularly drastic consequences. For example, by the mid 1970s hybrids had replaced almost all the open-pollinated Brussels sprouts used by commercial producers in Europe, and the same was soon true of cabbages and cauliflowers. The danger to traditional varieties of these crops is compounded by the fact that, rather than raise them themselves from seed, many gardeners buy brassica plants from garden centers or other stores, who in turn get them from commercial sources. So gardeners end up with the same few modern varieties as the main growers. Brassica seed is one of the most difficult types for small seed companies to maintain in production, because the plants occupy space over a long period and readily

COTTAGER'S KALE

Cottager's Kale is an old English variety of kale, raised in the 1850s. It was described in a contemporary gardening manual as '...4 foot high when fully grown, clothed to the ground with immense rosette-like shoots of a bluish-green tint, which, when boiled, become a delicate green.' It was easy to grow, and very hardy and productive, giving a useful harvest of young shoots in the spring months. Many growers considered it tender and fine flavored.

In the early 1990s EW King, the company who produced the seed in the UK, decided that not enough was being sold for it to pay its way. To generate a commercially viable quantity of new seed, plants of Cottager's Kale (a biennial) would have to occupy one acre of the company's land for two years. Also, kales cross-pollinate with each other, as well as with cabbages, cauli-flowers, and Brussels sprouts. To keep the varieties pure on a commercial scale, they have to be grown at least 1000 yards apart. A seed supplier such as Kings can only grow a limited number of brassicas for seed each year – so the best selling varieties must have priority.

Fortunately some dedicated individuals and seed saving organizations are continuing to grow Cottager's Kale; it is no longer available through any major commercial supplier in its country of origin.

cross-pollinate, so distinct varieties have to be grown in isolated cages, or separated from other varieties by substantial distances.

Now F1 hybrids are available for more crops than ever before. Nearly all corn in the US is from hybrid seed; almost all commercial growers in Europe use hybrid parsnips, for example, and the latest seed catalogs now even have new F1 hybrids of leeks and purple sprouting broccoli. The traditional varieties represent years of selection from growers and seedsmen, and as they disappear many valuable characteristics are undoubtedly lost.

This loss of cultivated vegetable varieties is tragic, yet the genetic diversity represented by cultivated food crops in Northern Europe and the US is relatively small compared to the huge diversity of landraces, and the wild ancestors of crops in all the major centers of diversity. The dramatic extinction of so many of these – in Central and South America, through Africa, India, China, to Eastern and Southern Europe – is potentially catastrophic.

Many indigenous farmers have been encouraged to abandon their many local strains of crops in favor of a few modern varieties, developed hundreds or thousands of miles away. These new varieties can be found in places as far afield as isolated Himalayan valleys, rural communities in Northern Russia, and in remote areas of the smallest African states. Even where the old varieties are still grown, they are often side-by-side with modern ones, so there is serious danger of cross-pollination occurring and contaminating the home-saved seed. In the Solomon Islands, for example, fine local varieties of small yellow watermelons, grown for generations by the subsistence farmers, have crossed with a larger imported hybrid variety; similarly, local purple maize has crossed with a commonly grown white sweetcorn.

The rise of the multinationals

It is only in relatively recent years that the seed trade has passed out of common experience into the hands of experts. Even 50 years ago farmers and gardeners routinely saved their own seed, and did amateur selection work to improve their own stocks. Their varieties were often taken up by small family-based seed firms, who also did their own plant breeding, and this work was complemented by public research institutes and universities. But in the 1960s this began to change, largely because of increasing sophistication in plant breeding techniques, and the rising use of oil-based chemicals in agriculture. Large multinational companies with primary interests in oil, chemicals, and drugs, began to invest in the seed industry, and many small firms without the same resources could not compete. Those that were not bought out were lost – and their seed lists, containing many unique varieties, often vanished too.

Throughout the 1970s and 1980s, the seed industry was in turmoil. In the US and Canada, in the three years from 1984 to 1987, over 20% of seed companies went out of business, or were taken over. The scene in Europe was similar. Until the 1960s Austria was a major seed-producing country, with many small breeders producing varieties adapted to the country's different climatic areas. Now there is only one main commercial seed company, and 95% of the vegetable varieties sold in Austria are imported. In the West, more than 500 family seed firms were bought out completely in the two decades between 1970 and 1990. Familiar company names may remain on the seed packets, but their owners are often the big multinationals.

As such companies have come to dominate the marketplace, so they have also become increasingly involved in research and development into plant breeding. It became US government policy during the 1980s to phase out federal research into plant breeding in areas where private companies could compete. In Europe, breeding work similarly shifted out of public hands.

The varieties that interest the multinational companies most are the new hybrids, bred to grow commercially in the widest range of climates and conditions, assuring highest sales. Many of the most significant losses are those varieties specifically adapted to local conditions – a large international company is unlikely to be interested in the low-volume regional specialties that were once the staples of the small seed companies they bought out. Varieties suited only to home gardeners, or to marginal areas, are the first to be dropped.

The chemical fertilizers or pesticides needed for the new varieties are often supplied by the same businesses that supply the seeds, a co-dependency which does not encourage the breeding of naturally vigorous pest and disease-resistant varieties. The links to chemicals are sometimes quite direct: among an increasing number of examples is the soya bean variety created by the chemical giant, Monsanto, which has been genetically engineered to tolerate their own glyphosphate herbicide (*Round-up*).

For large companies motivated solely by profit, it makes sense to concentrate on new hybrid varieties rather than traditional open-pollinated varieties; the seed from F1 hybrids will not come true to type, so farmers and gardeners cannot easily bypass the seed company by saving seed from their own crops. Even more significantly, newly developed (as well as newly '(re)discovered') varieties can bring companies extra revenue through registration of plant patents, and the application of plant breeders' rights.

ITALIAN VEGETABLES

Many of our most attractive heirloom vegetables come from Italy, where traditional ways of cultivating and cooking vegetables have continued remarkably unchanged for centuries.

Italian emigrants have spread numerous well known varieties far and wide across the globe. All broccoli varieties originally hail from Italy, as well as some leafy greens. A great diversity of beans, peppers, tomatoes, and eggplants have been cultivated for many centuries in the warm Mediterranean climate, as well as the onions and garlic so vital to Italian cuisine.

Ownership of genetic resources

In the past our vegetable heritage and the knowledge associated with it was regarded as a common resource. In the early 1960s, however, a number of industrial countries agreed on the concept of plant breeders' rights (PBR), by which a breeder could officially register a new vegetable variety and then receive a royalty from all those that use it.

The intention of this legislation was to reward plant breeders for their work, and to stimulate new research. Varieties protected by PBR could still be used without obligation by breeders to develop new ones, and farmers had the right to save seed from them for their own use. Unfortunately, the trend since then has been for increasingly restrictive controls on plant varieties.

The World Trade Organization now requires that Member States protect plant varieties by patents, or by an effective equivalent designed to fit the country's needs. The effects of patents are far-reaching: when plant genetic material is patented, the patent holder has sole rights over the material and every plant containing it. Under patent law, farmers and growers saving seed are liable to pay royalties on that seed. Similar restrictions apply to its use for plant breeding – another variety containing the patented genetic material would come under control of the original patent.

In the US, many plant patents have already been granted. They can be taken out not only on newly developed varieties, but on heirlooms that have not previously been named and marketed, so that large seed companies are gaining the rights to seeds that have been in families for generations. In Europe at present, plant varieties are not patentable as such. However, the scope of PBR has been widened so that farmers and growers no longer have an automatic right freely to save seed of varieties covered by PBR, and its use by plant breeders is already restricted.

Neither PBR nor patents take account of the rights of local communities and indigenous peoples. It is their skill and knowledge that developed the landraces and traditional varieties which are the basis of modern breeding programs. Varieties with desirable traits can be taken freely from countries in the centers of diversity by plant breeders in industrial countries, and used to create new varieties with the same traits. These effectively become the property of the large seed companies, and bring in revenue through patents or PBR. Often the varieties are sold back to the countries where the material originated, so, instead of being rewarded for their important contribution in developing them, the farmers may be required to pay to use the patented seed.

Farmers' Rights, arising from their efforts in conserving and improving the genetic resources in their own countries, have been recognized internationally, but are still undervalued. Any system of reward has yet to be implemented, and the whole question is the subject of on-going international debate. Taking out patents on their own resources is beyond the means of farmers and community groups, and it is often also against their spiritual and ethical beliefs.

It is also outside the scope of specialist plant breeders such as the small companies developing varieties for biodynamic growing. Many large companies are already spending considerable amounts of time and money in lawsuits defending their patents. Far from stimulating research, strict controls on access to genetic resources stifle innovation and threaten biodiversity. Our existing vegetable heritage has come about through the sharing of seeds and knowledge between individuals, communities, and countries far more freely than patents would allow.

Illegal vegetables

Besides the legislation governing PBR, the countries in the European Union have additional laws that control which vegetable varieties can and cannot be sold. No variety can be legally marketed unless it is registered on the National List of one of these countries. These regulations were designed to protect consumers from rogue seed traders, and to clear up genuine confusion, by ensuring that varieties were what they claimed to be. So carrot seeds from any packet labeled Autumn King must by law always produce plants of that variety. Similarly, companies cannot market Autumn King seed under the name of Charlie's Carrot or some other name of their own. In theory, these guarantees are desirable for seed suppliers and growers, but in practice the effect of the legislation has been reduction in choice through the loss of many old varieties.

When the system was first set up in the early 1970s, seed companies were invited to submit names from their catalogs for listing, and some old varieties were automatically included without charge. Many, however, were not. These included family heirlooms, and other varieties not commercially available in Europe. Hundreds of those originally listed have also since been dropped.

In 1980 a Common European Catalog was published, amalgamating the National Lists from all EC countries. Over 1500 varieties, said to be identical to others but registered under different names, were struck from the list. It has since been estimated that only about one-third of these were genuine duplicates, others were distinctly or subtly different. Once a variety was dropped, it became illegal to supply it, no matter how valuable it might be (*see Up-to-Date Onion, right*).

EXTINCTION

Agriculture has a nasty habit of changing relatively harmless organisms into major pests and diseases, by giving them crop monocultures, and removing natural predators. The best way to combat this trend is to produce resistant varieties by incorporating resistance from older varieties in modern ones.

It would be desirable, for example, to breed ringspot resistance into brassicas growing in certain areas, but this can no longer be done because the best source of ringspot resistance, the old Cornish cauliflower, was replaced by French material 30 years ago, and exists no more.

Possibly there may once have been mildew-resistant onions, aphid-resistant carrots, and clubroot-resistant cauliflowers ... extinction means we will never know.

UP-TO-DATE ONION

Bred in England almost a century ago, this strongly flavored onion is resistant to white rot – a disease affecting nearly all crops in the onion family. Up-to-Date was sold commercially in the UK until the 1970s, when it was dropped in favor of Bedfordshire Champion, to which it looked identical in trials. However, Bedfordshire Champion only appeared the same because there was no threat from white rot, to which it has little resistance.

Luckily Up-to-Date was kept in cultivation by a seed saving organization. Many other valuable varieties have not been preserved.

EGGPLANTS

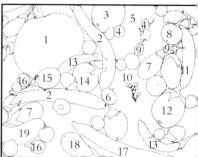

1. New York Spineless

2. Pingtung Long

3. Large White

4. Red Ruffled

5. Purple Pickling

6. Turkish Orange

7. Listada di Gandia

8. Laotian Green Stripe

9. Easter Egg

10. Laotian Grape

11. Long White

12. Rosa Bianca

13. Thai Green

14. Large White

15. White Oval

16. Ronde de Valence

17. Chinese Long Sword

18. Black Egg

19. Kurume Long Purple

Every variety on the market in Europe since the 1970s has had to be registered, requiring substantial fees, and strict testing. First it must pass a DUS test: it must be Distinct from all other varieties; it must be Uniform – all the plants of that particular variety must be the same, and it must be Stable – it must not change from generation to generation. Many old varieties, whilst being distinct strains, are not sufficiently uniform to satisfy the legislation.

The registration process itself is expensive, and there is an annual maintenance fee to keep the variety on the list. In the UK it costs around £1000 ($1500) to register a new variety on the National List, and £300 ($450) a year to maintain it there. These fees are the same regardless how many packets of the seed are sold, whether it is a kale bought by only a few gardeners, or a cabbage grown by commercial growers over thousands of acres. Small independent seed companies who would like to start selling re-discovered heritage varieties, or new varieties bred just for home gardeners, find that these fees make it completely uneconomic.

The zeal with which the letter of the law is enforced varies from country to country. Thompson & Morgan, one of the biggest companies in the UK supplying seeds to home gardeners, has been prosecuted and fined by the UK Ministry of Agriculture, Fisheries and Food (MAFF) for selling varieties that were not on the National List. These were giant vegetables – a cucumber, cabbage, carrot and pumpkin – which particularly interested gardeners entering produce in local shows and other competitions. The varieties had failed the DUS test because they were not sufficiently uniform: some of the cucumbers had white prickles and some had black; some of the cabbages had more red veining than others; the carrots varied too much in size for the Ministry's liking, and the pumpkins varied too much in color.

TM/M05 GREEN GRAPE TOMATO

Green Grape is a modern tomato variety, but it is nearly always considered an heirloom variety as it was selected (in the US) from a cross of an heirloom and a traditional variety (see Part Two, the Directory, page 163), and was released in 1986. The vigorous plants produce small cherry-sized fruits, with a delicious tangy flavor. When ripe, they are green with yellow veining, resembling Muscat grapes – hence their name.

In Europe Green Grape cannot legally be sold by name because it is not listed in the Common European Catalogue. Regardless of this, in 1997 it was introduced into the catalogue of the UK seed company Thompson & Morgan under the number TM/M05, and gardeners that buy seed receive a form to fill in about the variety's performance. This makes selling the seed legal because the tomato is 'under trial'.

MAFF also interprets the word 'market' in the legislation very strictly. At least one British company has been prevented from giving away unlisted seeds, inferring that this change of ownership of the seeds constitutes marketing. The main UK seed saving group, the Henry Doubleday Research Association, calls its seed collection a 'Library', with gardeners paying a membership fee but getting 'free' seeds; so far the Ministry has chosen not to prosecute. Other European countries appear to be more relaxed about the seed regulations, or to interpret them in different ways – unlisted varieties certainly feature in some Italian and French seed catalogs directed at home gardeners. But in general, the existence of the law is enough to prevent small companies from maintaining and selling unlisted heirloom varieties.

Nevertheless, there are ways of bending the rules. Reasonably large quantities of seeds may be distributed for trial purposes, so seed companies can put an unlisted variety in their catalog under a trial number, and ask customers to report back on its performance. Distributing seeds may be illegal, but distributing plants is not, and selling young plants of unlisted varieties through the post is becoming fairly commonplace. Even chitted seeds (seeds which have just germinated and have a small white rootlet showing) can be marketed.

Changes to the European law have been suggested – such as the creation of an official Heirloom List, or a list of varieties marketable in small quantities for gardeners, and there are signs that this may happen, but EC bureaucracy works painfully slowly. Meanwhile, each year more and more familiar open-pollinated varieties become outlaws: Cottager's Kale (deleted in 1992), Canadian Wonder French bean (in 1993), Sunset runner bean (in 1994), Hero of Lockinge melon (in 1995), Snow White cauliflower (in 1996)... and many more.

SAVING THE CZAR

When varieties have been cultivated by gardeners for decades it is usually for good reason, and the latest commercial varieties offered by the seed companies cannot always replace them.

This was certainly true of the Czar, a white-flowered runner bean with long, almost stringless pods, introduced in the UK at the end of the 19th century. It had enduring popularity with gardeners, possibly because it had white seeds which were very good for drying as well as tender fleshy pods. It featured in seed catalogs for nearly 100 years before, in 1988, it was threatened with deletion from the National List. It took a determined campaign by the Henry Doubleday Research Association to persuade one seed company to save it.

As a consequence the Czar is now legitimately undergoing a revival as an heirloom variety, but others have not been so lucky. The melon Hero of Lockinge was introduced by the seed firm Carters in 1881 as the 'finest new melon of the season'. It has beautiful yellow fruit, with flesh that is almost white and very tender – one of the varieties grown in the melon houses of Victorian kitchen gardens, remaining a favorite for over a century. But in 1995 it was dropped from the National List. Now it is illegal for anyone to sell the seed.

ORIENTAL GREENS

Oriental Brassicas, Pak Choi and hardy Mustards are among the fast-growing Oriental vegetables which provide a wide choice of fresh salad and stir-fry greens when other leafy vegetables are limited.

Industrial food production

The combination of modern farming methods and the nationwide marketing of fresh produce has meant an inevitable concentration on fewer vegetable varieties. Whereas previously farmers would have produced a wide mix of crops over a long harvest period, increased mechanization and the use of chemicals make it much easier, and more profitable, for them to grow large areas of a just few varieties.

In most industrialized nations only a small proportion of fresh produce is marketed locally through small greengrocers or farm shops. Many farmers now grow to the demands of the largest foodstores, which have taken over an increasing share of the market from greengrocers. The major foodstores want to buy large quantities of a uniform crop at a specified date, and are not interested in any variety that is only grown in small amounts, or that does not travel or store well. In order to satisfy these demands, farmers increasingly grow a narrow band of crops which ripen uniformly, all look the same, and are easy to harvest with minimum labor by machine.

As more food is sold in a ready-to-eat form, the demands of the food processors also have an influence. Whereas at home we adjust recipes, oven temperatures, and cooking times to suit a great variation in produce, processors match their machinery and production lines to a few suitable varieties, further limiting the number which they find acceptable. So it is the food processors, not growers or consumers, who are important in determining which potatoes are planted, for example, as only a few varieties are suitable for them to make crisps or oven chips.

As consumers, it is all too easy to get caught up in the system, to buy washed and prepacked vegetables because they are eye-catchingly displayed, and to use pre-prepared and pre-cooked dishes because they are quick and simple.

Cooking a meal used to mean taking fresh raw ingredients and turning them into a dish, but this happens less and less. To many people, the communal meal and the traditions and values associated with food appear, sadly, to be less and less important. Some have never been taught to cook the commonest vegetables, let alone squashes or salsify. The food processors and supermarkets decide what they eat, and hence what the farmers grow, and how.

In developing countries, modern farming methods and associated development such as roadbuilding and damming, have had drastic consequences for genetic diversity and local communities. As fields are enlarged and chemicals introduced, not only are traditional varieties displaced but native wild plants in the field margins are destroyed. These include many which are important to the local diet and culture. Peasant farmers, who cared for the old varieties for centuries, are turned off their lands so that the landlords can increase their acreages. High value 'cash crops' for export are often grown in preference to local crops.

The effects can be startling: for example, the area round the Aral Sea is part of the Central Asian center of diversity, the home of many melons, onions, garlic, carrots, radishes, turnips and other crops. The Aral Sea was once the fourth largest inland sea in the world, but during the 1930s all the rivers flowing into it were diverted to irrigate monocultures of cotton, grown with high levels of chemical inputs. Now the Sea has lost 60% of its surface. The soil on the exposed dry sea bed contains dangerously high levels of pesticides and salts, and these are blown around in desert dust storms, contaminating plant and animal life for hundreds of miles around.

CHILE BEANS AND TACOS

Following the 1995 Rio conference on Biodiversity, one environmental group, SAFE Alliance, published a paper illustrating how traditional agriculture maintains diversity, whilst modern food production systems work against it. This is one of their examples.

Beans and tacos form a meal that can be bought, ready-made, in many foodstores. It is also a typical main meal of Mexican peasants. However, everything about the way the two meals are produced is different.

The Mexican peasant grows the maize and the beans together and the tomatoes and chiles at the side, in a mixed cropping pattern that makes best use of the soil nutrients and minimizes the spread of pests and diseases. Several varieties of each species are used – each with differing resistance to variations in climate and to pests and disease, so whatever the conditions, some of the crop will provide a good yield.

Industrial agriculture grows separate large areas of maize, beans, tomatoes, and chiles, each area containing a single variety; chemical fertilizers are applied to supply nutrients and pests and diseases are controled by spraying. The food manufacturer buys in the four genetically uniform ingredients in the world market so that each of the ingredients might conceivably even come from a different continent.

Modern marketing

Farmers in developing countries can often be persuaded that the up-to-date seeds which come with outstanding promises are superior to their traditional local varieties, which quickly become something to be ashamed of. Representatives from some major companies are eager to capitalize on this attitude.

Seed Savers International (SSI) is a project run by Seed Savers Exchange which supports a network of plant collectors in Eastern Europe and the former Soviet Union. During the fall of 1993, one SSI plant collector, working in many remote villages in the mountains of Southern Poland, continually ran into sales representatives from the giant seed company Cargill, selling rye and other agricultural seeds door-to-door, inviting farmers to change from their traditional tried-and-tested crops.

In Europe and the US, many gardeners are similarly lured by glossy catalogs and glowing descriptions of the latest varieties. In mainstream gardening circles, growing the old favorites is often viewed as unfashionable and backward-looking, and saving seeds from last year's plants to provide for next year's sowings is considered by many as eccentric, or in some places it is even seen as an indication of poverty. Yet for our ancestors it was an integral part of the cycle of growing their own food, and of developing new varieties.

It is not necessary to turn the clock back, so that everyone must save all their own seeds. But neither can the process be left to a few multinational companies. More people – small seed companies, individual farmers, growers, and gardeners – with varying interests and different ways of growing plants, need to be involved in seed production and plant breeding. Only then will diversity be maintained and our food supply become less vulnerable.

POSITIVE GROWTH

ABOVE: *The diversity of sweet potatoes is so great that some varieties will even thrive in cooler climates.*

LEFT: *Asparagus appears as the harbinger of summer in any garden, an early and delicious treat after the winter months.*

The main official response to the threat of lost genes has been to collect endangered varieties and put them into long-term storage in gene banks. One of the first and most important collections of such genetic material was assembled by the Russian botanist Vavilov and his colleagues. Their travels to collect plants during the 1920s and 30s in particular led Vavilov to identify the centers of diversity of our crops (*see page 21*), and made him fully realize the importance of preserving them. The Vavilov Institute of Plant Industry in St Petersburg has more than 360,000 seed samples from countries around the world.

In 1943 Vavilov died in a Soviet prison, a martyr to his scientific beliefs, and many of his colleagues also perished under Stalin's regime. Stories of heroism abound: apparently up to 14 scientists died at their desks at the Institute during this period, starving to death rather than eating any of the edible seeds around them, which they saw as indispensable resources for the future. Their work was, and still is, a source of inspiration to other scientists.

Many countries worldwide have now set up gene banks, some housing predominantly local varieties, others carrying a range of crops from a wide area. The Nordic gene bank in Sweden, for example, concentrates on varieties from the Scandinavian region, whereas the UK gene bank maintains world collections of radish, onions, carrots and many cultivated brassicas. In the US, the National Seed Storage Laboratory (NSSL) houses nearly 400,000 seed samples from recent and traditional varieties, and from wild species, of all the main crops grown in North America.

Gene banks store seeds under cold dry conditions. Seed is typically dried to 5% moisture content, hermetically sealed in foil packets, and stored at -20°C (-4°F). Under these conditions, the seeds of some vegetables will remain viable even after 25 years, although their potential to germinate will gradually decrease. In the NSSL, some seeds destined for long-term storage are packed into small tubes and their temperature lowered to -160°C (-256°F) using liquid nitrogen.

Periodically the seeds must be grown out: a proportion of the seed of each variety is sown and grown, then new seed is collected and returned to the bank. Some crops can be grown out in nearby open plots, but others must be kept in glasshouses, or isolated in tunnels covered with insect-proof netting to prevent cross-pollination. Potato varieties must be grown from seed potatoes rather than botanical seed to keep them true to type, so they have to be stored as tubers in a cold-room and regenerated annually, or kept under laboratory conditions in tissue culture.

This hi-tech solution to saving our vegetable heritage is one important approach, but it has some major drawbacks. Collections in gene banks inevitably only represent a sample of what actually exists in cultivation and in the wild. Sometimes the selection is deliberate, focusing on immediate rather than long-term solutions – varieties are specifically sought for characteristics that are commercially important at the time, such as a specific disease resistance. Other seed collecting missions, although more eclectic, are very often limited by time or money, or by the social or physical conditions in the areas where they take place.

Gene banks can only be as safe as the technology upon which they rely – some are in areas with unpredictable electricity supplies, for example – and they are also vulnerable to deliberate sabotage and accidental damage. In recognition of this, collections are usually, but not always, duplicated in more than one gene bank in more than one country. The Nordic gene bank has also set up a secure long-term store which does not rely on a power supply – in a steel container deep within an abandoned mine gallery in Svålbard within the Arctic Circle. The gallery has a 230 foot thick roof and a naturally stable temperature, generally between -1°C (14°F) and -4°C (25°F).

However, by far the greatest danger to gene banks is lack of government funding, and lack of clear policies for the future. In Canada, 1995 budget cuts closed or curtailed the activities of some of the country's gene banks. In underdeveloped countries the funding is likely to be precarious. Many European gene banks suffer from lack of resources, and even the NSSL, the US's most important collection of genetic material, is dangerously underfunded. This means that seed samples are not being grown out or evaluated as often as they should be. Seeds are dying in storage. There is a need for clear international agreement, and consistent funding.

Another problem in gene banks is preserving the genetic diversity in the stored seeds. The number of seeds grown out to renew a sample that is deteriorating will only be a small percentage of those originally collected, and is unlikely to represent the full genetic picture. For example, an initial sample of the seed of wild potato species stored at the Scottish Crops Research Institute might contain enough seed to generate about 20,000 plants, but only about 40 are used to regenerate the sample.

Some seeds will also store better than others, and some plants will do better than others when grown out – in conditions which may be quite different to those in the region where the seed sample was collected. Thus, as time goes on, varieties adapt to conditions in the gene bank, rather than evolving to meet changes in the environment, or in pest and disease organisms in the outside world.

Gene banks are one vital resource in conserving biodiversity, but they are the preserve of scientists and at the mercy of government policies. Conservation is also vital at the grassroots level, on farms and in gardens, and there is now increasing awareness of this. International organizations, individual countries and states, and, in particular, pressure groups and local communities, are all responding. On many fronts positive action is being taken. It is beginning to make a difference.

Field and garden conservation

When an unexpected outbreak of wart disease struck UK potato crops in 1910, inspectors noticed that amongst the many varieties in cultivation the variety Golden Wonder was immune. From this variety other resistant varieties were bred. If only a few varieties had been growing, and the rest had been kept in gene banks, the chances are that a variety with this valuable trait would never have been discovered. It is essential to maintain vegetable diversity where it belongs – in gardens and on farms. Then crops will naturally adapt and evolve, and we can assess how they perform under a wide range of conditions.

This value of diversity, and the importance of local farming and gardening methods in preserving it, is at last beginning to be recognized, particularly in the developing world, where local attitudes are moving away from the ideas of the 'Green Revolution' (*see page 48*). In such countries there is often a great diversity in traditional crops, and the problem is to dispel the myth that what comes from outside is better.

One of many successful initiatives has taken place in the Chiloe Islands, off Southern Chile. These are considered to be one of the centers of origin of the potato, but over the last few decades local varieties have gradually been displaced by modern ones. In an attempt to halt this loss of the traditional crops, in 1989, a community-supported 'living gene bank' of native varieties was planted. Within a few years seed potatoes from this program were being distributed to farmers, who quickly discovered the advantages of the old varieties: they do well under a wide range of conditions, taste better, and use less fuel to cook. Now, rather than relying on external initiatives, the farmers are selling and exchanging seed amongst themselves.

NATIVE SEEDS/SEARCH

Native Seeds/SEARCH (NSS) is a not-for-profit organisation working to collect rare, wild, and heirloom Native American plant species and varieties. NSS' stated mission is to 'conserve and promote the use of native or adapted agriculturally valuable plants, and to establish through research their cultural, nutritive and ecological value'.

NSS store and distribute the seeds of these native plants, both locally and globally. While the seeds are available to any interested growers, Native American groups receive seeds free of charge; this is the NSS way of thanking the thousands of original seed-savers, the native tribes who nurtured indigenous species, and preserved them, keeping their culinary traditions and folklore intact.

In addition to gifts of seeds, NSS organizes and participates in education and cultivation programs, and actively encourages the native peoples of the South West to grow their traditional native seeds. These are adapted to the desert, the mountains, and poor soils. Many native species naturally tolerate droughts and pests and diseases, and in the less-than-ideal conditions of the arid South West, native seeds will always outperform modern non-adapted varieties.

WINTER SQUASHES

1. Longfellow
2. Futtsu
3. White Cushaw
4. Early Large Yellow Paris
5. Rouge Vif D'Etampes
6. Ucon Acorn
7. Striped Cordebese
8. Candystick
9. Gold Striped Cushaw
10. White Acorn
11. Whangaparoa Crown
12. American Indian
13. Tatume
14. Tarahumara Indian
15. Mandan
16. Campêche
17. Fordhook
18. Triamble

Seed savers' networks

It is often personal experience that prompts people to action, to keep alive the link between plants and people, and resist the loss of our vegetable heritage.

In 1970 Diane Whealy's grandfather gave her and her husband Kent the seed of three plants that his family had brought with them to the US from Bavaria four generations before. These were two vegetables – a large German tomato and a prolific climbing bean – and a beautiful dark strain of the flower Morning Glory. The old man, Grandpa Ott, died that winter, and Kent and Diane realized that it was up to them to keep the heirlooms alive. Kent then began to write to gardening magazines in an attempt to locate other people who might be keeping seeds passed to them by their families, and from this small start grew the Seed Savers Exchange (SSE), the largest seed savers' network in the world, with 8,000 members dedicated to saving endangered vegetable varieties. Their companion Flower and Herb Exchange fulfils the same role for flowers and herbs.

In the UK, it was the insidious progress of plant breeders' rights and the seed regulations that rang alarm bells to one man – Lawrence D Hills. He was founder of the Henry Doubleday Research Association (HDRA), an organization established to research and promote organic growing (now Europe's largest), and under their auspices he campaigned for the country's vanishing vegetables and launched a Seed Library to make heritage varieties available to gardeners and growers throughout the country. To the 7,800 members of HDRA's Heritage Seed Programme, Lawrence Hills cries to 'Save the Czar', a traditional white-flowered runner bean (*see page 49*), and other vegetables which were about to be dropped from the National List, are now legendary.

Michel and Jude Fanton started Seed Savers' Network in Australia when they began to search for particular varieties and found they were not available through any recognized seed supplier in Australia. Advertisements in gardening magazines provoked such a great response that the Fantons were inundated with offers of seeds and information. So they decided to share this wealth with other gardeners, while continuing to build up reserves of heirlooms from every possible source.

In Austria, Nancy Arrowsmith runs the seed savers' network Arche Noah (Noah's Ark), now the only privately owned seed supplier in Austria. And in The Netherlands, the Court of Eden encourages people to grow as many varieties as possible from their extraordinarily diverse collection of seeds.

As well as acting as seed suppliers and as seed banks, Arche Noah and Seed Savers International – a SSE project – have jointly arranged several expeditions to collect endangered vegetables in Eastern Europe and the Mediterranean. Over the last few years losses of traditional varieties have been occurring in these genetically rich areas at an alarming rate, and the national gene banks in most of the countries concerned are not in a position to do any collecting themselves, with few facilities and limited funding for the maintenance of varieties.

These and the other seed savers' networks that grew up in the 1970s and 80s have various features in common which distinguish them from official gene banks. They do not collect seeds according to currently relevant criteria, such as the specific needs of industrial agricultural systems, but collect and receive as wide a range of varieties as possible. Rather than collecting in order to store seeds away for some future date, networks want to make the seed available to everyone – they want the seeds to be used. Through growing the seeds, using the vegetables, saving some seed each year and redistributing it, gardeners will bring the old varieties back into common use.

The members of seed savers' networks in Europe and North America between them maintain and exchange thousands of varieties of traditional vegetable varieties. For example, the 1997 yearbook of Seed Savers Exchange lists about 12,000 traditional varieties and the addresses of 1,000 members who are offering these to other gardeners. Some of these varieties are family heirlooms, others have particular historic value; most are not available at all from commercial catalogs.

Sometimes remarkable heirlooms have simply turned up in the post. When Jeremy Cherfas was running HDRA's Heritage Seed Programme, he described how one morning he received a bulky padded envelope containing not seeds, but two turnips about to run to flower. A note inside from the sender of the rather smelly package said that the turnips were an old commercial variety called Laird's Victory, kept going for decades by his neighbor who had recently died at the age of 90. The seeds had been thrown out by relatives clearing up – all that remained was the turnips in the garden.

Often, however, it has taken a more determined search to find heirloom varieties. The investigations of the Swedish seed saving group SESAM led to the discovery of six local landraces of fava bean (broad or field beans), although the Nordic gene bank had only one. Peter Erlandsson of SESAM also describes how he rescued a local grey pea variety from a province in the South of The Netherlands. The 11 seeds which he obtained were about 40 years old – but 10 of them germinated, so the stock could be renewed. Other Swedish heirlooms have been repatriated to SESAM from the US via Seed Savers Exchange (*see above, right*).

ESTHER'S SWEDISH BEAN

This drying bean is an heirloom from a family that emigrated in the 1800s from Sweden to Montana. It is a vigorous hardy plant, which thrives in cold climates, and produces a good crop of brownish yellow beans.

This variety disappeared completely from its native country earlier this century. However, it was kept in cultivation by the Seed Savers Exchange, and eventually it was repatriated to the Swedish seed savers' network SESAM.

BRASSICAS

1. Long Island Improved
   Brussels sprouts

2. Andes cauliflower

3. Sicilian Purple cauliflower

4. Evergreen Ballhead cabbage

5. Siberian kale

6. De Cicco broccoli

7. Georgia collards

8. Early Purple Vienna
   kohl rabi

Alternative markets

Even if you can't grow your food yourself, you can increase the choice of what you eat by buying direct from farmers and market gardeners. Marketing vegetables directly to consumers allows growers to produce small quantities of a greater range of crops and varieties, and vegetables do not have to travel, or look perfect.

There are now over 2,400 local farmers' markets in the US, and it is estimated that over 4 million consumers get a portion of their fresh produce from them. They offer the chance to buy fresh locally grown food, and to try out produce not found in stores. Much of Europe has a long and thriving tradition of local vegetable markets, and you can also buy direct from the producers in other ways.

In the UK, there has been a huge rise in 'vegetable box schemes' during the past few years. Under these schemes, fixed price boxes of organically grown seasonal produce are delivered directly to customers. Generally one grower, or a group of several local growers, will produce nearly all the produce to fill the boxes, and a close relationship builds up with the customers. This offers the chance of growing what people want, and the opportunity for growers and consumers to try something different.

Another exciting way forward is the rise of community supported farms, a more radical way to become involved with those who are growing the produce. Community members contribute financially directly to the farm by buying a share in the produce before it is grown, and participating in decisions about what is grown. Throughout the US the number of such projects is growing steadily. They nearly always result in an increase in the range of what is grown, and make the members more aware of the intrinsic value of diversity.

CHEFS AND RESTAURANTS

Restaurants can play an important part in raising the profiles of traditional vegetables. All over North America, and in Europe, chefs are increasingly using traditional vegetables. The first chefs to make the heirloom statement were, not surprisingly, in California, where you can now find a number of superb restaurants using little but heirloom varieties. They have made the public aware of, for example, the numerous varieties of garlic, eggplants, and squashes, and heirloom vegetable and flower salads are increasingly popular. In France, one prestigious hotel chain with restaurants in and around Paris, has actively helped to save varieties such as the Green Paris artichoke (Gros Vert de Laon), popular in the last century but shunned in recent years because it is less productive for market gardening than modern counterparts. The century-old cabbage Chou de Saint-Saëns, has also been recently rediscovered and taken up by local restaurants.

One fine restaurant on Vancouver Island in British Columbia uses only seasonal produce grown within a 30-mile radius. Their dishes include many local plants eaten by the American Indians, such as the flat-leaved nodding onion (Allium cernum), and Indian celery (Lomantium nudicale), as well as other traditional crops. One favorite is the Gourgane bean, a local fava bean with very thin-skinned beans.

Small seed companies

Although the pressures described in earlier chapters have dangerously depleted resources, regeneration of interest in our heritage is encouraging the growth of a number of small seed companies selling open-pollinated and endangered varieties. The situation in North America is more optimistic than anywhere else. Here, with a bit of sleuthing, you can find fascinating heirlooms of most vegetables. Some suppliers dedicate themselves to saving and marketing varieties of one species – several specialize in tomatoes and peppers, or beans, corns, or squashes. One individual, Ted Mackza, (the Fish Lake Garlic Man), declares himself dedicated to making Canada 'self-sufficient in garlic'; other growers are equally proud of their own specialties.

At the time of writing, legislation in Europe makes the marketing of old varieties more difficult (*see Chapter 3*). Nevertheless, an increasing number of small companies are seeking out and selling legal traditional varieties, or finding ways around the laws. There are also hopeful signs that legislation may soon be changed to allow more varieties to be legally sold.

A number of small seed companies are now specializing in selling 'biodynamically' produced seed. Biodynamics is a system of growing put forward by the German philosopher Rudolf Steiner – a type of organic growing which recognizes the energy cycles of plants and the role of cosmic forces. There are no hybrids in the biodynamic catalogs, and many contain old regional varieties which were developed before the advent of chemicals in agriculture.

If you support the small specialist seed companies, and buy varieties that are endangered by modern hybrids, these varieties are much less likely to disappear.

HIGH ALTITUDE GARDENS

This small family-run company has been trading for over a decade; it is one of the longer established bio-regional seed companies, promoting the growth of varieties suited to particular climates and conditions. Situated at over 5,000 feet in Idaho, surrounded by snow-capped, towering peaks, High Altitude Gardens focusses naturally on the challenge of gardening in harsh climates.

They find and grow vigorous, short-season varieties from around the world, acting as a resource for thousands of gardeners looking for diversity and reliability. Many of their varieties are equally suitable for less extreme climates.

HAG focus primarily on open-pollinated varieties, but many of the varieties they offer are also heirlooms.

UNDERWOODS SEEDS

One of the growing band of dedicated small seed suppliers, Maryann Underwood started her seed saving network and business from home after a serious accident left her unable to continue her previous work. Starting with some of the seeds she had saved herself, and through trading with members of Seed Savers Exchange, it was not long before people were sending her seeds, and she now has a huge variety of heirloom seeds, particularly tomatoes.

Members of Underwood Gardens receive preferred ordering for rare or limited quantity seeds, but anyone can order from the catalog.

SEEDS

A handful of bean seeds is a geat illustration of vegetable diversity. All colors and sizes are here, with varieties suitable for cool climates, hot areas, fresh eating, shelling, slicing, or drying. Bean seeds are easy to save and store, and many varieties will still germinate after several years' storage.

Living museums

Many seed saving organizations have gardens where you can see heritage vegetables growing. SSE has a 170-acre farm in Iowa, which includes an orchard and wildlife conservation area, as well as a garden where around 1,500 vegetable varieties are grown annually for seed.

Positive steps are being taken throughout North America to preserve the pieces that make up our agricultural heritage. Hundreds of living museums now exist. Some of these, such as the Living History Farms in Des Moines, Iowa and the Museum of American Frontier Culture in Staunton, Virginia, provide historic re-creations of agriculture and food production from earlier times. Others, such as Old Sturbridge Village, Massachusetts, have recreated the whole way of life for a community, where the gardening and farming practices play crucial roles. These living museums pay rigorous attention to the types of plants that would have been grown at relevant periods, as well as the methods, and can often be a good source for heirloom varieties of vegetables, herbs and flowers.

Living museums offer the opportunity to observe methods and cultures of farming from earlier times. They also provide a very immediate way of informing an increasingly urbanized population about contemporary issues concerning food production. Many of the issues discussed in earlier chapters are immediately brought to life when confronted with the obvious practical diffences in the traditional and the new methods of farming and land use.

Whereas museums can re-create the traditional methods, they cannot re-create traditional conditions, and the traditional varieties which are cultivated have to adapt to modern conditions (pests, diseases, climate); it is this interaction of the old and the new that helps to maintain and develop diversity.

THE NATION'S MOST FAMOUS FARMER

The Thomas Jefferson Center for Historic Plants has recreated the well documented garden of the nation's most famous farmer, at Monticello in Virginia. Thomas Jefferson's vegetable garden was a 300 yard long, southeast facing terrace, where he experimented with different crops including hundreds of different varieties from many countries. At one time he cultivated 15 varieties of English pea, for example, as well as many native plants.

Jefferson recorded his gardening activities in the first part of the 19th century in great detail. A diary exists describing his daily sowing and harvesting, as well as a 'garden book' with cultural notes, and many letters that he wrote.

Extensive research has gone into locating the types and varieties of vegetables he grew, and the Center is a good source of seed of the heirloom varieties known to have been originally cultivated. Even if you can't visit the garden in person, you can become a member of the Center and receive fascinating newsletters and a seed catalog.

Community events

There is no better way to become aware of our endangered vegetable heritage than to see and taste the varieties. With this in mind, numerous events are organized by local communities and seed saving groups, and even if you have no garden at all you can become involved.

Every October, Seed Savers Exchange hosts a Pumpkin Celebration at its Iowa farm, where pumpkins in many different shapes and sizes are available for carving. There is a huge bonfire, a dinner, and a procession with lighted pumpkins. Among other vegetable-oriented festivals, Native Seeds/SEARCH holds a pepper fiesta, and there are well attended garlic festivals in Europe and California. Your area might have other celebrations. Seed Savers Exchange also holds an annual camp-out, with lectures and other events, a great way to meet other seed savers and hear the latest news and views.

In the UK, the HDRA hold a Potato Day where over 100 varieties of rarely available seed potatoes are on sale. Tubers are priced individually instead of being packed into two pound bags, so even if you only have a small garden, you have the opportunity to try lots of different varieties. Potato Day also includes talks, cookery demonstrations and displays of the old varieties from HDRA's Heritage Seed Programme.

At a local level, a simple way to introduce heirloom varieties is to enter them in horticultural shows or bring them to similar community gatherings – pot luck suppers, bring and buys, harvest festivals. They may not win any prizes, but will certainly attract plenty of attention.

Events which focus on regional history and culture can also be a focus for traditional crops. For example, twice a year the Ecomusée in the town of La Corneuve in France holds its Marché au Musée, selling over 70 varieties of fruit and vegetables, all currently grown in the region. La Corneuve was once part of the largest vegetable producing plain of France (La Plaine des Vertus) where many regional varieties arose. These figure prominently in the market alongside modern introductions, and many dishes based on recipes from old cook books are prepared for people to taste. The Marché au Musée encourages people to try traditional varieties, and hence helps persuade commercial producers to keep them in cultivation.

GARLIC FESTIVALS IN FRANCE

The French have been cultivating garlic for centuries, and there are many customs associated with it, particularly in the South-eastern part of the country. Here it is traditionally planted on 10th November, and harvested on 20th June, and festivals associated with garlic occur at different venues in Provence throughout the summer.

The Foire de Saint Jean in Marseilles is the first of many, at the end of June, and many locals buy their garlic supply for the year during the fair, but possibly the most celebrated garlic festival takes place at the end of August at the town of Piolonc in central Provence. The surrounding area is reputed to grow the best garlic of all, on fertile plains below the rocky slopes, in fields intersown with strips of lavender.

Producers gather from all over Provence, tractors pull decorated trailers full of garlic around town, pavements are edged with strings of garlic bulbs, the whole town smells of garlic and local herbs as regional specialties are prepared in cafés and on pavements, and chefs race each other along the main street. All the local varieties are on sale – and for sampling – at stands throughout the town, but the old favorites continue to be the traditional pink-striped Rose de Lautrec, and the very large-bulbed white Blanc de Lomagne.

⑤

SAVING THE SEED

ABOVE: *Purple-podded pole beans came from France in the 18th century. They are hardy, productive and adaptable.*

LEFT: *Alliums growing for seed in one of the Preservation Gardens at Seed Savers Exchange in Iowa.*

Few gardeners now save seed of their own crops, yet this is the link which enables traditional varieties to be widely grown and heirlooms to be passed from generation to generation. Seed saving does not have to be complicated, and for many crops it is very easy, particularly those where the fruit or seed pods are also the edible part of the plant, such as tomatoes and beans. There is little difference between growing these crops for seed and growing them to eat – the main difficulty is usually stopping the family from picking them all!

Some climates pose limitations on growing certain crops for seed, particularly short-season areas, or where weather is unreliable, but, with a few years' experience, it is possible to grow seed from most vegetables in most areas.

Saving the seed of some crops departs slightly from normal vegetable growing routine. You may need to grow crops in different places in the garden, for example, to isolate them from one another. You may need to leave them in the ground for much longer than you would to get an edible crop, and they may take up more space – a lettuce grown to eat is small and compact, but when left to seed it will send up flower stalks about 3 feet tall. Seed production will depend largely on the size of your garden, on the climate, and on how much time you can spend gardening.

It is usually possible to save seed from the majority of common vegetables without much difficulty, although brassicas and sweetcorn pose particular problems. This short chapter aims to show you what is involved in seed saving, and to get you started with one or two easy crops. For detailed crop-by-crop information, you will need a more specialized book, and some are recommended in *Further Reading (pages 183-186)*.

Begin seed-growing with your favorite varieties, those which have proved to be well adapted to your environment, and to your own personal taste. Be warned, seed saving tends to be addictive – once you start, you will almost certainly want to do more. It is fascinating to watch plants that you do not normally see flowering run up to seed. Some of the seed heads – the white umbels of the carrot, for example, and the architectural spheres of the leek – are also wonderfully attractive, and are loved by bees and other beneficial insects.

Above all, it is extremely rewarding to have seed from your own crops to sow next year, and extra to give away to friends and neighbors.

Annual, biennial, or perennial

One of the important characteristics you need to know about a vegetable before you consider saving it for seed, is whether it is annual, biennial or perennial.

Annual crops are those that are started from seed each year and produce flowers and seeds within one season of growth. They are usually sown in spring and give seeds in the fall - which fits in well with the growing cycle in the vegetable garden. Lettuce, peas and spinach are just a few of the many crops that come into this category. Where the growing season is short, some annual crops may need to be grown in a greenhouse or tunnel in order to produce seed.

Biennial crops are those which do not go to seed until their second growing season, after a period of winter cold. Biennials include most of the winter brassicas, spinach beet, leeks, onions, and roots such as carrots and parsnips. It takes eighteen months or more to produce seed from these crops. Roots and onions often need to be lifted and stored over winter, and replanted the following spring. Leafy crops are best left in place in the garden, although this is a problem in cold climates where winter temperatures can be too low for them to survive.

Perennial crops are easy to maintain as they do not have to be propagated from seed each year. They include those that grow on in the same place year after year such as asparagus, globe artichokes, sea kale and tree onions, and those which we dig up from the vegetable plot each year, but which are propagated from tubers or offsets – potatoes, Jerusalem artichokes, garlic and shallots, for example. These last crops are particularly easy to multiply and pass on, but they run the risk of accumulating virus diseases. Some plants, such as peppers and tomatoes, are actually perennials but are treated as annuals in most climates.

Keeping the variety pure

In order to produce seed, a flower must be pollinated: the stigma of the flower (the female part) must receive pollen from the anthers (the male part) either of the same or a different flower. Some crops self-pollinate – pollen is transferred within the same flower resulting in fertilization. Others cross-pollinate – pollen is brought from another flower, usually by the wind or by insects. If the pollen comes from a different variety of the same crop species, then plants from the resulting seed will be a cross between the two varieties and not true to type.

In peas and beans self-pollination occurs before the flowers even open, making saving pure seed particularly easy. Peppers will also self-pollinate, but in addition cross-pollination by insects often occurs. If you are growing more than one variety of pepper, you must therefore take steps to isolate the varieties in some way to ensure pure seed. Brassicas are the most outgoing; most have a mechanism that prevents self-pollination, and for a flower to set seed it must have pollen brought by insects not just from a different flower, but from a flower on a different plant. One brassica plant on its own, even if it has many flowers, will produce little if any seed.

Separation distances

If you want to save seed from two varieties of the same species flowering at the same time, they must be separated by a distance large enough to prevent contamination by insects or wind-blown pollen. It is not only pollen from your own crops that you have to consider, but that from your neighbors' crops, and possibly from weeds of the same botanical family. Carrots will cross with wild carrots, for example, and cabbages, cauliflowers, broccoli, kale, Brussels sprouts, and kohl rabi will all cross-pollinate with one another, and with some field brassicas and their escapes in the wild.

Necessary isolation distances vary widely from crop to crop. Bush (or French) beans, which self-pollinate and rarely cross, only need a minimal distance of a few metres between two varieties to keep the seed pure. Cabbages, on the other hand, usually need to be separated from similar flowering brassicas by around 500 metres; commercially distances of around a kilo-metre are required. The minimum distances will also depend on other factors such as how many insects there are around and what else there is for them to feed on. Obstacles between crops such as hedges, buildings, and other barriers can also reduce the chances of cross-pollination.

Physical barriers

An alternative to isolating crops by distance is to use physical barriers. If you require only small amounts of seed it is simplest to cover individual flowers or flower clusters with a bag. Use paper bags or pieces of horticultural fleece, never polythene bags, as these create a hot humid atmosphere and encourage the flowers to rot. Alternatively, whole plants or even groups of plants can be caged to keep out pollinating insects. It is easy to make cages cheaply from wood covered with window screen mesh or screen wire.

Remember that since both bags and cages keep out insects, flowers inside them that are not self-pollinating will normally need pollinating by hand. Or you can stop two varieties that are growing alongside one another from cross-pollinating, and yet still allow insects to work them, by caging them on alternate days. Whilst the first is caged, insects can pollinate the second and vice versa. Swap the cages at night.

Selecting plants

Always save seed from as many plants of a variety as possible, even if just one would give enough seed for your needs. Otherwise there is a risk of decreasing the genetic diversity within the crop. Some vegetables are more sensitive to this danger than others. Those that usually self-pollinate, such as tomatoes, lettuce, peas and beans have little natural variation within any one variety. You could successfully save seed from just a couple of plants – although it is preferable to use about six. At the other end of the scale, crops such as sweetcorn and onions deteriorate markedly if seed is saved from too few plants. At least 20 onions and 100 corn plants of any one variety are needed for seed saving, otherwise its variability will be lost and undesirable traits may appear.

You also need extra plants to allow you to select the best, and to 'rogue' out any which are not true to type or have unwanted characteristics. You should always choose vigorous healthy plants for seed saving, but other criteria for selecting 'the best' are not always as straight-forward. You need to look at the whole plant, not just the part you eat, and consider such characteristics as pest and disease resistance, drought resistance, resistance to bolting, and harvest time. For example, the first lettuces that produce flower spikes are not the ones to select, however tempting that may be, because the seed saved from these plants will probably give lettuces that also bolt early, giving only a short harvest period.

If you are maintaining an heirloom variety, you will want to choose the most typical plants to use for saving seed, so that their characteristics will be passed to future generations.

Seed collecting and cleaning

Fruiting crops that have seeds embedded in moist flesh must be harvested when the fruits are fully mature. For pumpkins, this is the same stage as you pick them for eating, but for cucumbers and zucchini, you must leave the fruit on the plant for much longer than you would for a normal harvest. Scoop the seeds from the mature fruits into a large container of water, stir them vigorously to remove pieces of flesh, then rinse them in a sieve. The seeds of some fruits, particularly tomatoes and cucumbers, are often put through a natural fermentation process (*see page 96*) before cleaning, to destroy any seed-borne diseases that might be passed on to the next generation of plants.

Crops that produce seeds in pods, husks, capsules, or any dry casing should be left on the plant until they are completely dry. If wet weather sets in, pull up whole plants and hang them in a dry airy place. Check seeding plants regularly – the seeds of some crops fall to the ground when they are ripe, so you need to harvest gradually over a long period to avoid losing them. The ripest seed umbels of a carrot plant, for example, may need covering with a paper bag in windy weather to collect fallen seed.

Your harvest will be a mixture of seed and 'chaff' – the pods and other debris, which should be separated and discarded before storage. Lightly roll or crush the mixture inside a bag or sack – the simple equivalent of a threshing machine – to separate the seeds from their cases. 'Winnowing' – separating the chaff from the seeds – was traditionally done by the wind, but a hair drier works fine. Shake small amounts of seed in a bowl until the debris collects at the top and then lightly blow it away. Alternatively, you can sieve the chaff from the seeds, or vice versa. Don't worry if your winnowing is not perfect!

Drying

It is essential that seeds are dried quickly and thoroughly before you store them, otherwise they may start to germinate or go mouldy. Small podded seeds that were harvested dry usually need minimal further treatment, but large seeds, and those harvested wet from fruit, need a longer drying time. A good air flow, rather than a high temperature, is the most important factor. Direct drying in the sun or oven can be damaging. Dry small quantities of seed in a large bowl on a shaded windowsill, stirring occasionally, or hang them in paper or netting bags in a warm airy spot. Label them with the variety name, origin, and date of harvest; good record keeping is invaluable when you are saving the seed of heirloom varieties.

Storage

Seeds store best in a cool, dry, dark place where there is little temperature fluctuation. What seem like obvious places to put them – in the garden shed or on the kitchen shelf – are often the most unsuitable.

One effective way to create dry conditions for small quantities of seed is to keep them in paper packets in an airtight container with some silica gel crystals. Silica gel (available from most drugstores) takes up water from the atmosphere inside the container and from the seeds, turning from blue to pink as it does so. You can then dry it in a very low oven until it turns back to blue, and put it back with the seeds. Use one teaspoonful of crystals per ounce of seeds.

Store the jars of seeds in a cold place – a spare room or, ideally, in the refrigerator. Do not put them in the freezer unless you are confident that they are thoroughly dry. If seed moisture levels exceed 8%, their walls can be damaged as the water inside them freezes.

ABOVE: *In summer the Preservation Gardens at SSE are a patchwork of color – here they are trialing varieties brought back from Eastern Europe.*

Most vegetable seeds will keep well for around three years if stored properly – but the time does vary from crop to crop; parsnip seeds, for example, are difficult to keep for longer than a year, whereas squash seeds can keep up to ten years. If you have more seed than you will use, give it away to friends and neighbors, or join a seed savers' network and pass it on. The more people that grow and appreciate heirloom varieties, the more likely they are to survive.

SIMPLE SEED SAVING

TOMATOES

Tomatoes self-pollinate and are one of the easiest crops to save for seed; that is why we can find such a wide selection of heirloom varieties. Cross-pollination hardly ever occurs, except in some of the oldest varieties such as currant tomatoes (*L. pimpinellifolium*). Even then, this should not be a problem unless you are growing several older varieties alongside one another.

Leave the fruits on the plants until they are really ripe, then cut them open and squeeze out the seeds and gel into a bowl. Leave the mixture in a warm place for several days, until a layer of mould covers the surface. It will smell very unpleasant, but it is worth putting up with this because the natural fermentation kills many seed-borne tomato diseases.

After 3 or 4 days scoop off the top fungal layer and use a sieve and clean water to wash the seeds. Tip them onto a plate or tray, and dry them in a warm place out of direct sunlight.

GREEN BEANS

The numerous varieties of bush and climbing green beans are annual plants which self-pollinate, and are very easy to save for seed. Cross pollination rarely occurs, but as a pre-caution, do not grow two varieties that you are saving for seed right alongside one another. Separate them by a few yards and/or grow another tall crop in between.

PLANT SELECTION:
When the plants are young, remove any with discolored foliage or any other sign of disease. When some flowers and pods have formed, select about six plants with typical characteristics to save for seed. Mark them clearly so that no-one picks their pods to eat.

COLLECTING SEED:
Ideally, the pods should be left on the plant in the garden until they are completely dry. However, once they have turned from green to yellow/brown, you can safely pull up the whole plant and hang it upside down in a warm dry airy place – the seeds will continue to ripen. Do this is if wet or frosty weather threatens.

CLEANING:
Pod small quantities by hand. Put larger quantities in a sack, and tread all over it or beat it to split the pods and separate the seed. Remove the pods and other debris by hand or by blowing with a fan or hair drier.

DRYING:
Dry the seeds thoroughly in a warm airy place. Hang them in paper bags or thin hessian sacks, or lay them thinly on a drying tray made by stretching some fine mesh material across a wooden frame. Test whether the seeds are dry enough by hitting one or two with a hammer. They will shatter if dry, but squash if further drying is necessary.

Pumpkins and Winter Squashes

Pumpkins and winter squashes may belong to any one of several species, all of which look superficially very similar. They are annuals, and differ botanically from most other vegetables in that they have separate male and female flowers on the same plant. The female flower has a distinct swelling at the base, whereas the male flower is on a long straight stem.

The flowers are very attractive to bees, and varieties of the same species will readily cross-pollinate within a distance of about 500 yards. However, the blooms are large and easy to isolate and pollinate by hand.

PLANT SELECTION:
Growing six plants of any one variety is usually considered sufficient to maintain genetic diversity within the variety (although ideally you need twelve or more). However, this should not stop you from saving seed from fewer plants for a year or two if that is all you have room for. To pollinate a female flower on one plant, use male flowers from several other different plants.

HAND POLLINATION:
In early evening, find male and female flowers that are due to open the following morning. This is easy to determine with practice – the flowers begin to show a flush of yellow and may start to break open at the tip. Tape the tips of these blossoms shut with masking tape, or cover each of them with a piece of horticultural fleece, well secured where it meets the stem. In the morning, cut off the male flower, remove the tape or fleece and all the petals so that the anthers are exposed. Remove the tape or fleece from the female flower and open it gently; rub the anthers of the male flower onto the stigma in its center. Re-tape or cover the female flower, and put a tag on the stem so that you can identify the fruit that you have pollinated when it is mature. Soon the flower will wilt and any cover can be removed. If pollination has been successful, the fruit will then start to swell.

COLLECTING SEED:
Harvest the fruits when they are fully mature, and then store them for a few weeks to allow the seeds to plump up. Cut the fruit open, and scrape out the seeds into a bowl.

CLEANING:
Add water to the seeds and rub them to remove any remaining pieces of flesh. Collect the seeds in a sieve.

DRYING:
Put seeds on a flat surface in a warm dry airy place. They are dry enough for storage when they break cleanly into two pieces if you try to bend them.

PART

2

*The Directory of
Heirloom Vegetables*

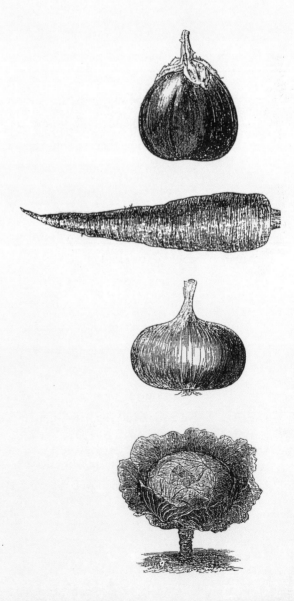

The **Directory** is not intended to be a definitive guide to heirloom varieties. Its purpose is to point you in the right direction, to indicate some well-loved and highly recommended varieties among the diversity of vegetables that are available for you to try. Equipped with this volume, you can throw away all conventional seed catalogs from huge commercial suppliers, and buy seeds instead from the dedicated band of seed suppliers and growers who are working to ensure that a genuinely wide range of open-pollinated heirloom vegetables is available to every home gardener. You will be rewarded with a garden full of interesting plants with fascinating histories, and above all, fantastic flavors. Once you've started heirloom gardening, you will probably be hooked for ever!

Heirlooms, for the purposes of this volume, are largely those vegetables which have been preserved through the actions of a family or community, rather than maintained by commercial seed companies. We have also included some traditional varieties which are definitely worth growing and preserving – these are varieties with historic value which have survived for many generations; they may have been commercial varieties at some stage.

There is an ongoing debate among some gardeners about bio-regionalism : one side suggests you should concentrate on growing only those plants that originate from your area, that are part of your region's culture, and are adapted to your soil and climate, even to your microclimate; the other side suggests that the introduction of non-local varieties of plants enriches an area's ecology and culture. Where there are truly local varieties, which are part of your local ecosystem, and traditions, do try and find them, grow them, and maintain them. But most vegetables are much traveled; do not be afraid to try some old variety that hails from some entirely foreign country, it may also be perfectly suited to your particular bio-region, as well as to your palate, and there may be important cultural links.

Where the most suitable climates/areas of the country for growing specific varieties are not indicated in the profiles of vegetable varieties in the **Directory**, the crop will succeed in most places. However, bear in mind that long maturity crops are unlikely to be suitable for areas with short growing seasons. Don't be put off: it is worth trying almost anything, almost anywhere, and if you get interesting results pass them on to your seed supplier, local seed exchange or network. Many heirloom varieties have become endangered during the last decades, and there is not always a lot of information about their behavior in different areas/soils/climates, so any details you can provide are valuable.

We have tried to give some indication of growing times, of cultivation requirements, and climatic preferences. But

don't be downhearted if something that is listed as requiring
63 days to maturity seems to take longer in your garden, or if
the taste is slightly different to what you were anticipating
from the description. These things do vary from area to area,
from soil to soil, and season to season. We have provided the
basic information that will help you to enjoy choosing and
producing fine and flavorsome vegetables for your homes,
and your seed suppliers will be able to give more details if
you have any further questions about your particular soil and
location. Don't be afraid to ask, people who are growing
heirloom varieties are a helpful bunch, only too keen to
spread the word further!

In general, we have indicated the number of days to
maturity from seedling stage, as germination times can differ
according to the ways you start your seeds. For direct-seed-
ing crops, we have indicated the length of days from seed to
harvest. Where we haven't provided any information about
growing times, this is because results differ so much from
area to area that it would be misleading or even unhelpful to
suggest a precise period.

To give you some easy indication of where you can
obtain specific seeds, codes at the end of each heirloom
vegetable profile point to specific suppliers for that variety.
However, space has limited us to a few recommendations per
variety, and seed suppliers' lists change from year to year, so

send off for catalogs from suppliers listed in the **Resources** section which follows the **Directory**. Here you will find many valuable addresses for suppliers of open–pollinated and heirloom seeds, and gardening organizations. The seed catalogs make fascinating and inspiring reading, and some-where, there will be the perfect varieties for you. Use the specialist suppliers, join campaigning organizations, and find out from gardening friends and neighbors about other local groups. If there are none within reach, why not start one yourself? Although heirloom gardening comes out of the past, it is vitally concerned with the present and the future, and the more people that are involved, the better it will be for all of us, and for the world we live in.

Try and save some seed from your gardening adventures, use it the following season, and pass it on to friends and neighbors. Then you, too, will be helping to preserve vital resources for future generations while enjoying the wonder-ful flavors of these old–time vegetable varieties. And if you are inspired to know and grow more, join Seed Savers Exchange; they will be able to put you in touch with growers and seed savers nearby – and far away.

What is most important is that you should enjoy your heirloom gardening. We hope that **Part Two** will give you the inspiration and information that you need to get started.

USDA HARDINESS ZONES

*Throughout **The Directory** temperatures are stated in °C and °F, rather than referring to the standard USDA Hardiness Zones. If you need to check the minimum temperature in the Zone where you live, or a neighboring Zone, use the chart below. Remember that many factors apart from minimum temperature affect the ability of a plant to survive – these include the amount of wind, rain, sun, snow cover, humidity and soil, as well as altitude, exposure or shelter, and proximity to water sources.*

ZONE NUMBER	CENTIGRADE	FARENHEIT
1	below -45°C	Below - 50°F
2	-45 to - 40°C	-50 to -40°F
3	-40 to -34°C	-40 to -30°F
4	-34 to -29°C	-30 to - 20°F
5	-29 to -23°C	-20 to -10°F
6	-23 to -17 °C	-10 to 0°F
7	-17 to -12°C	0 to 10°F
8	-12 to - 7 °C	10 to 20°F
9	-7 to -1°C	20 to 30°F
10	-1 to 5°C	30 to 40°F

Contents

BEANS

Phaseolus vulgaris, P. coccinus, P. lunatus, Vicia faba

All *Phaseolus* species of cultivated beans came originally from Central and South America, but have adapted and naturalized worldwide. They were probably domesticated in ancient times before being introduced to Europe and Asia after the Spanish conquest. Beans are usually classified as snap, shell, or dry, depending on the stage they are best eaten. Snap or green beans are picked fresh and whole from early summer onward, when the seeds are undeveloped or very small. Shell or horticultural beans are slipped from their pods when they are fully formed but not yet dried out. Dry beans are harvested when they rattle in the pods. Most dry beans make good snap beans, and quite a few are good as shell beans.

Bush beans are known as French beans in Europe, where they are eaten fresh, sliced in the pod, and more rarely used dried. Fast-growing annuals, they mature early, and most varieties are highly productive. Bush beans will grow in any well drained garden soil as long as they are not planted out until the soil is warmed, and all dangers of frost are long past. Pole beans are typically high-yielding and make more efficient use of space than bush beans, but are often later maturing. Beans need a minimum temperature of 65°F (18°C) to germinate well, and need nitrogen during the first three weeks until their nitrogen-fixing nodules develop.

Fava beans, or broad beans, *Vicia faba*, came from Europe with Columbus, and thrive in cool rainy areas. Use them as frost-tolerant spring planted beans from Virginia northward, plant in the fall in southern and gulf coast states. Use as a snap bean harvested at 2-3 inches long and as a shell bean when pods are 4-7 inches.

Runner beans, *Phaseolus coccinus*, are perennial beans originally from Central America. Many runner varieties can be traced back to the Hopi Indians before the arrival of the Spanish, and they may even have been cultivated by the Aztecs. However, Europeans took them back from the New World and adapted them to shorter daylight hours and short season growing. White-seeded varieties have white flowers; red and purple-seeded varieties have red flowers. Pods will not set in high temperatures – over 90°F (32°C).

Beans will flourish if the soil is fed with plenty of nitrogen-fixing organic matter, or injected with an inoculant available from many seed suppliers. Dark-seeded varieties are more resistant to rotting than light-seeded.

Most dry beans are self-fertile so you don't need to isolate varieties. However, fava beans can be insect cross-pollinated, while runner beans cross readily with any other runners, and Lima beans, *Phaseolus lunatus*, are also susceptible to crossing. Rotate beans in your garden on a 3-year cycle. Never cultivate or harvest them when the foliage is wet for fear of spreading rust diseases or blight, and never walk through wet bean plants – this is one of the commonest ways of unwittingly spreading disease.

DRY OR SNAP BUSH BEANS
....

Phaseolus vulgaris

Jacob's Cattle / Trout / Dalmatian   **85-95 days**
This beautiful maroon and white heirloom has been
around for centuries, and is particularly popular in
short-season areas – New England and the North.
The seeds are distinctive, kidney shaped spotted
with maroon markings on a white coat. Jacob's Cattle
is an excellent baked bean and good for soups.
Cooks, FloMo, Goodseeds, SaltSpring, Shumway

Ireland Creek Annie's   **60-75 days**
Exceptionally high yielding, these tan-colored beans
were believed to have come from Ireland in the 1850s.
This variety is good for wetter areas, as it is fairly resis-
tant to rot. Use dried for baking.
AbuLife, DeepDiv, SaltSpring

Hutterite   **75-85 days**
This heirloom came from Austria via Canada to the US
in the 1750s. It is probably the best soup bean of all,
its plump light green seeds dissolving rapidly to form a
delicious creamy-white soup.
AbuLife, Landis, Synergy, SaltSpring

Black Valentine   **48-70 days**
Excellent snap bean dating back to the 1850s with
slender stringless straight pods. It germinates well in
cool soil so is good for early plantings. Dependable
and prolific, it is resistant to bean mosaic.
AbuLife, Cooks, Landreth, Shumway

Midnight Black Turtle   **90 days**
This variety makes a good fresh snap bean, and is
good for soups, stews, and refries. If you are short of
space, grow this one, as it has an abundant pink
flower display, rather than commoner white flowers.
AbuLife, SaltSpring

**Wren's Egg / London Horticultural /
Taylor's Dwarf Horticultural / Shelley /
Speckled Cranberry Egg / King Mammoth /
Araucano**   **85 days**
A semi-runner bean whose pale green pods are
streaked with red, opening to reveal beautiful pinkish-
buff seeds splashed with carmine with a dark orange
eye. This ancient pink-flowered variety from the Andes
came to the US from Italy, and is adapted to be
productive from the North to the Deep South.
Extremely attractive, pick young for snaps as these
beans become stringy with age.
AbuLife, Ontario, SaltSpring, Verbean

Hopi Black   **70-90 days**
Small prolific bushes give reliable yields of tasty beans
which can be eaten snap or dry. The beans are small
and black, and Hopi Indians used to use them for dye
as well as for food.
AbuLife, DeepDiv, Native

Montezuma's Red   **85-100 days**
This brick-red bean was once grown by the Aztecs,
and beans have been found in 3,000-year-old burial
grounds. Very productive and tolerant of soil and
weather conditions, it puts out semi-twining branches
on bushy 14 inch plants. This is one of the best dry
beans for baking as it doesn't get soggy.
AbuLife, DeepDiv, Nichols, SaltSpring

Low's Champion / Dwarf Red Cranberry   **68 days**
One of the oldest known New England heirlooms, this
has flat 4–5 inch pods and beautiful mahogany seed.
Beans are delicious as snaps when young, and are also
good as green shell beans or dry.
AbuLife, Johnnys, Shepherds, Synergy

Pencil Pod Black Wax   **52 days**
A long and reliable producer, even in hot dry areas,
these stringless snap beans are good fresh or canned.
AbuLife, SaltSpring

Dragon's Tongue   57 days

A unique Dutch wax bean, producing long, creamy yellow pods which are covered with thin purple stripes. A prolific producer, excellent flavored beans are terrific fresh or dried.

AbuLife, DeepDiv, Greenseeds

DRY OR SNAP POLE BEANS

Phaseolus vulgaris

Cherokee Trail of Tears / Cherokee Black   85 days

These beans were carried by the Cherokee Indians on their forced march westward, when displaced from their land by white settlers in the 1800s. Long lavender flowers precede slender pods which turn a dark purple with small black shiny beans inside.

Fox, SaltSpring, SESE, Threshold

Kentucky Wonder / Old Homestead /
Texas Pole / Egg Harbor   60-75 days

A very reliable and productive early maturing variety. Green-podded beans are good fresh, canned, frozen, or dried. This variety is rust-resistant.

Butterbrooke, Goodseeds, Pinetree, SESE

Blue Lake Stringless   60-65 days

An outstanding early and prolific variety with long green tender rounded pods produced throughout the summer. Their very sweet taste make them favorites for fresh eating, canning, and freezing.

JLH, Liberty

Oregon Giant   65 days

Broad and thick light green pods are attractively streaked with purple. One of the favorite old varieties in the Northwest, lush everbearing vines thrive in cool weather.

Garden, JLH, SOregon

Pole Romano / Italian Pole /
Italian Green Pod Pole   60-70 days

A delicious gourmet bean, vines produce tender long brown-seeded beans over a long season. When young the pods are edible, and these beans are good for canning, freezing, or eating as fresh shell beans. Back in the 1950s this bean was so unpopular that, although it was available, the seed stores that stocked it did not even bother to put a picture of it on the packet. It took off for the home gardener and became the most important home freezer bean because it is stringless, and soft and delicate. After only 2 minutes' cooking it has none of the usual crispness or sharpness which is associated with many other string beans.

Comstock, Dam, DiGiorgi, SESE

Lazy Housewife   85-100 days

An old German variety introduced to the US about 1810. It was so named because these were the first snap beans that did not need de-stringing. However it may have been first grown in the US as **White Pole**. Late season white flowers are followed by fleshy stringless pods containing white beans mottled with grey. An excellent dry bean.

Landreth

Blue Coco / Purple Podded Pole   59 days

A French heirloom, pre-1775. Fleshy purple pods contain meaty chocolate seeds. Blue Coco will produce under almost any conditions, even when hot and dry.

SESE, SSI

Rattlesnake   75 days

Known in some parts as Preacher bean, as it is so productive it is something to preach about, strong climbing plants produce cascades of 8 inch rounded pods which can be harvested early for very sweet snap beans or left for dry beans. Pods are purple streaked, like the skin of a rattlesnake, and beans are buff, speckled with dark brown.

FedCo, Fox, Pinetree, Verbean

Genuine Cornfield   **85 days**

One of the oldest known varieties of cultivated beans, traditionally grown between rows of corn. Vigorous plants bear an abundant crop of 6–7 inch tender round pods on tall vines. Use these beans dry.
DeepDiv, Fox, Redwood

FAVA OR BROAD BEANS

Vicia Faba

Aquadulce   **75 days**

One of the most popular English heirloom varieties, it gives good yields of medium-sized Windsor type beans. This is the best variety for an early crop and can be planted in fall or from January on as it is very tolerant of cold.
AbuLife, SESE

Bunyard's Exhibition / Conqueror   **65-75 days**

Another tasty bean from Northern Europe. This variety is consistently reliable and very well-flavored; each pod contains 7 medium-sized beans.
AbuLife, Verbean

Broad Windsor Long Pod   **85 days**

A traditional English variety, producing exceptionally well in cool climate areas. Beans are tender and plants crop over a long period. Try and pick them small as the beans tend to toughen as they get larger.
AbuLife, Dominion, SESE

Red Cheek   **70 days**

A very old Peruvian variety, presumably developed from European varieties post-Columbus, as Favas originated in the Mediterranean. Moderate-sized green or tan beans have purple blotches, and no two plants have beans with the same markings.
DeepDiv

RUNNER BEANS

Phaseolus coccinus

Scarlet Runner / Best of All   **70 days snap**
100 days shell

The most popular green bean grown in England for around 250 years. This pole bean variety was discovered in South America in the 1600s, and taken back to England in the 1700s; it was then reintroduced to America the same century, but was already being grown there by early colonists who had obtained seed from the Native Americans. The bright scarlet flowers attract hummingbirds. Good for table and ornamental use, harvest it as a snap bean when young and tender.
Goodseeds, JLH, Landreth, Pinetree, SESE, Verbean

Painted Lady   **75-85 days snap**
100 days shell

This rare heirloom was first recorded in the US in 1855. Beautiful red and white blossoms make this plant brilliant in the border, and it produces fine flavored beans in 9–12 inch pods, good fresh or for freezing.
Aimers, Bountiful, SaltSpring

Scarlet Emperor   **65-90 days**

Deemed the best runner bean in the UK at the beginning of the 20th century, dark green pods grow up to 15 inches long, but remain tender. Very easy to grow, these beans can be picked over several weeks.
Bountiful, Cooks, Territorial

LIMA BEANS

Phaseolus lunatus

Henderson   **65 days**

These buttery beans were found growing wild along Virginia roadsides after the Civil War. Plants are compact, with glossy dark green leaves, producing small pods with 3–4 small seeds in each. They appear drought-resistant, bear over a long season, and beans have a good flavor.

DiGiorgi, Meyers, Pinetree, Redwood

Christmas Pole Lima   **80-85 days**

Large, beautifully speckled red and white beans are delicious fresh, canned, or frozen. This variety yields particularly well in hot and humid conditions.

Fox

Jackson Wonder   **65-75 days**

Vigorous and productive plants bear curved pods containing buff seeds splashed with deep violet. This is an old favorite variety which is very tolerant of heat and drought.

Gurneys, Shumways, Verbean

Baby Bush   **70**

Small bushes bear large crops of short pods over a long season. Plump white beans turn gray-green when cooked, they have a good flavor and have been popular since the Civil War.

Burgess, Cross, Greenseeds

BEETS

Beta vulgaris

Until the 1880s beets were known as 'blood turnips'. There are no definite records of beet before the 16th century, but they come from the same family as Swiss chard. Sugar beets are grown widely as a source of sugar, and many varieties of beets are cultivated as animal fodder; table varieties can be sliced and pickled, baked, boiled, or eaten raw. Most beets are best eaten young as they tend to toughen with age.

Plant for fall or winter harvest in July, keeping soil uniformly moist to ensure germination. Beets need a deeply dug bed because of their long taproot. Grow them in light loam, in a light but not hot position; keep them moist and cool as hot weather beets can get tough and stringy. If the soil is too rich beets are liable to turn to seed, or get forked roots. Careful watering at early stages helps to prevent ring formation in the root.

If you intend to leave beets in the ground for the winter you should provide a 6 inch straw mulch to prevent the ground from freezing. Beets are susceptible to scab which causes brown spots on the skin; prevent this by making sure the soil is well drained and well balanced and practice good rotation.

Early Wonder — 50-60 days

Introduced to the US in 1811, this fast-growing variety produces succulent greens as well as smooth-skinned ball-shaped roots which taper slightly. Use the tender tall tops for greens and the dark red roots for salads, pickles, bortsch, or sliced cooked beets. Plant in early spring or early fall for continual harvest
AbuLife, DiGiorgi, Earlys, SESE

Golden Beet — 60 days

One of the sweetest of all beets, the attractive bright golden roots are very fine textured. Popular in Europe for centuries, these beets are best fresh, but store well and are great for pickles.
Gurneys, Nichols, OrnEd, Territorial

Chiogga / Dolce di Chiogga — 52 days

When you slice this early Italian beet it reveals striking red and white concentric rings, particularly decorative and tasty in salads. When cooked, the circles merge to an overall pink color. Tops are green with pink-striped stems. Less fussy than some varieties, Chiogga competes well with weeds to produce reliably.
AbuLife, Pinetree, SESE, Synergy, Verbean

Winter Keeper — 75-80 days

This sweet tender variety grows vigorously, and holds its greens well into the winter if mulched heavily. Very dark red, the roots taper slightly.
AbuLife, Comstock, Stokes, Territorial

Lutz Beet — 75 days

Lutz can get very large but never loses its sweetness. Plants produce copious amounts of very succulent greens, and this variety is good for overwintering in coastal and southern locations.
HighAlt, Pinetree, SaltSpring

Long Season — 80 days

Grow this variety if you want beets for storage. Large deep red roots stay sweet and tender through months of storage in moist sand in a cool place. They are just as good at the end of winter as at the beginning!
Cooks, JLH, Gurneys

Feuer Kugel — 70 days

An old European heirloom with smooth-skinned perfectly round roots. Sweet and tender to a large size, the skins slip off easily when cooked.
Turtle

Detroit Dark Red — 60 days

Introduced to the US in 1892, this developed from the popular European Early Blood Turnip. It has an excellent flavor and is mildew-resistant. This dark red beet has very dark green foliage with some red coloration.
Fox, Ledden, MacFayden

Crosby Egyptian — 50 days

A refined version of the Egyptian Beet brought to the US in the 1860s from Germany. 3–5 inch roots are deep red, turnip shaped and rapid growing. The flesh is very tender dark vermilion red. This is a good early variety, and stores well.
Fox, Gourmet, Shumway, Verbean

BROCCOLI
Brassica oleracea var *botrytis*

Originating in the Eastern Mediterranean, broccoli traveled to Italy in the 17th century, and from there to Northern Europe where it was sometimes called Italian asparagus. Italian immigrants brought broccoli to the US and made it popular.

There are two types of broccoli: the oldest type is sprouting broccoli, developed from European wild cabbage; this forms a medium-sized head and numerous small flowering shoots which can be picked over a long season. Standard or heading broccoli, sometimes referred to as calabrese, forms one dense head, which may be purple or green. Calabrese varieties do not always form sideshoots after the head is picked.

Like all brassicas, broccoli likes rich moisture-retentive soil, but is more sensitive to hot weather than most. It is a cool weather crop, tolerating low temperatures to 20°F (-5°C) but may split when cold-injured.

Start seeds inside in early spring for summer crops, or in late summer for late fall or winter crops, transplanting when the seedlings have sprouted 4-5 leaves. Broccoli can be direct-seeded if soil is warm and moist.

Most diseases can be prevented by rotation – don't grow members of the cabbage family in the same spot year after year. Cutworm infestation can be avoided by placing a heavy paper collar around plant stems as you set them out. Cover the crop with a floating row cover to help prevent flea beetles and root maggots.

Calabrese / Early Italian   60-90 days
Dark green plants have large blue-green central heads that appear until frost. Once these are cut tender side shoots are produced abundantly for several months.
Bountiful, Fox, JLH, Pinetree

Romanesco / Roman Broccoli   85 days
This variety has an attractive large pale green whorled head, made up of spiraling florets like a minaret or seashell. Originating in Northern Italy, Romanesco is good for salads and dips as well as steamed or boiled, and freezes well. Good for Northern areas, sow this in early summer for a fall crop.
Aimers, Earlys, JLH, Pinetree, ThoMo

Rosalind   60-65 days
An early purple broccoli, which is adapted to maturing during the heat of the summer, but performs best in cooler fall weather.
Territorial, ThoMo

Purple Sprouting   220 days
The traditional Northern European variety: cold-hardy biennial plants overwinter before heading in March/April. Growing 2-3 feet tall, plants are covered in small sweet-tasting purple heads which turn green when cooked. This is a must for northern gardeners!
AbuLife, Cooks, Territorial, ThoMo

De Cicco   65 days
Popular in the last century, De Cicco has a tender central head and numerous side sprouts. You can use the young leaves like kale or collard greens.
Comstock, Fox, Goodseeds, OrnEd, SESE

BROCCOLI RAAB
Brassica rapa

Often known as Italian turnip, or turnip broccoli, this is non-heading broccoli, where the tops and flower shoots can be used as a leafy vegetable. Grow like broccoli as a tender and delicious source of early spring greens in milder climates.

Spring Rapini / Broccoli Headed Turnip / Sparachetti   **40-70 days**

Plant this old European variety early in the spring and harvest the tops and tender flower shoots before the hot weather.

Dominion, Landreth, Stokes

Di Rapa   **85 days**

This non-heading European variety produces a huge crop of turnip-like leaves, slender flower stalks, and small flower heads that can be eaten as salad greens, or cooked. Sow this variety in early fall or early spring, picking just as flower buds start to open. It is a favorite winter vegetable in Italy.

JLH, OrnEd

BRUSSELS SPROUTS
Brassica oleracea var *gemnifera*

Believed to have originated in the 14th century near Brussels in Belgium, sprouts developed from a form of wild cabbage, and are an excellent cool-weather crop. Their unnecessarily bad reputation seems to derive from bad cooking! They are delicious lightly steamed, or opened and stir-fried.

Sprouts need a long growing season (85–100 days minimum) but they are very frost-tolerant and survive well in northern gardens. They are best picked after frosts, when they develop their sweet flavor. In cool climates sow in spring as early as the soil is workable. Pinch out growing tips as the sprouts develop to encourage a heavy yield. In milder climates start plants in late summer and overwinter them, protected by mulch, to pick sprouts from November through March.

Rubine Red   **95 days**

A highly attractive example of the red type available since the 1930s. Very ornamental, this variety is a reliable producer and extremely frost-hardy.

Aimers, Bountiful, Pinetree, Verbean

Catskill / Long Island Improved   **85-110 days**

The standard old favorite, an early and very productive semidwarf variety. Well known for its fine flavor, heavy yields, and hardiness, Catskill is widely grown.

AbuLife, Dam, JLH, SESE

Bedford Fillbasket   **85-100 days**

This old-fashioned English variety produces large solid sprouts from September through December. Sturdy plants are about 4 feet tall.

DeepDiv, Seedschange

CABBAGES
Brassica oleracea var *capitata*

Domestic cabbages developed from wild cabbage whose cultivation spread from the Middle East into Europe and Asia thousands of years ago. The earliest cultivated types were loose-headed, similar to modern Savoy cabbages, but smooth-headed varieties have been grown for several hundred years, with red and purple varieties popular in Europe since the 16th century.

Cabbages generally need cool weather to form good heads, and plants tolerate light frosts. They grow best in a deep rich loamy soil. As seeds need warmth to germinate, start them off indoors in early spring, planting out as soon as your soil can be worked. For best results brassicas need about 60°F (16°C) at the seedling stage – if it is much hotter the seedlings tend to get leggy. For fall or winter harvest you can sow seed directly into the garden 2-3 months before the first frosts. Most varieties of cabbage will store well in cool, well ventilated areas.

Protect against pests and diseases by careful rotation; use a row cover to avoid flea beetles; avoid yellow root rot by keeping plants well mulched and watered to keep soil temperatures cool. If you want to save your own seed, remember that cabbage is a biennial, only producing seed the second year, and each species of brassica can be cross-pollinated by insects, particularly by bees. Either grow only one variety at a time, or grow some especially for seed at least 400 yards away from others.

GREEN CABBAGES

Brunswick   **85-90 days**

This old-fashioned drumhead type has uniform sized broad flat heads which store well. This variety is very climate tolerant, and is one of the best cabbages to grow in hotter areas, although yields will be lower than when grown in a cooler climate.
JLH, Garden, Glecklers

Early Jersey Wakefield /
True American   **60-75 days**

Originating in England in the late 1700s, **Early Jersey Wakefield** has been cultivated in the US since the 1830s. An early conical-headed variety, it has a mild sweet flavor. Most gardeners grow this for summer harvest, but it will overwinter well without splitting, and is very slow to bolt.
FedCo, FloMo, JLH, Nichols, SeedsBlum, Verbean

Marner Allfroh   **60-70 days**

A versatile old German variety of small garden cabbage. Sow in spring to get very solid heads of medium size, or sow in May/June to harvest small, tennis-ball size heads with a very delicate flavor.
Bountiful

Slava z Enkhuizen   **105-115 days**

A traditional East European cabbage, brought back from Poland by Seed Savers International. It grows very prolifically even on poor soils, producing firm round pale green heads of about 6 pounds, which are good fresh and great for sauerkraut.
SSI

RED CABBAGES

Red Rock — **100 days**
Solid round red heads have fine flavor and keep well. This variety is well adapted to most climates and is great for cooking, salads, or pickling.
Baxter, Meyer

Red Drumhead — **60-70 days**
Round, slightly flat deep purple heads should be harvested at about 7 inches diameter. This is a very sweet-flavored cabbage, delicious raw as well as cooked. Plant in the early spring to harvest in fall, or grow this as a reliable winter keeper.
Bountiful, Landreth

Red Danish — **95 days**
This fine quality red cabbage produces very tight 6–8 pound heads which store exceptionally well, losing none of their flavor and remaining crisp and dense.
Heirloom

Red Acre Early — **80 days**
A highly recommended short-season red cabbage. Deep reddish purple 2–4 pound heads are very round and solid even in the early stages, with a very good flavor. This variety is very reliable, especially in northern states.
AbuLife, Gourmet, Gurneys, Shumways

SAVOY CABBAGES

Savoy Perfection — **90 days**
Compact short-stemmed plants have round flattened heads of heavily crumpled leaves. Crisp, firm, and very good mild flavor, particularly after a light frost.
JLH, Landreth

Savoy Drumhead — **85 days**
Leaves are thick and coarsely crinkled (savoyed) to form dark gray-green heads. Typically 4–5 pounds, these are very crisp and strongly flavored.
AllSterLot, Fox, Landreth

Chieftain Savoy — **80-105 days**
This very hardy variety reliably produces large firm round flattened heads. Leaves are dark blue-green and finely curled, white inside and very good fresh or after storage. Plant in summer for late fall or winter harvest.
AbuLife, Shumways, Territorial, Verbean

January King — **140-210 days**
Popular in Northern Europe for over a century, many gardeners consider this the best of all winter cabbages. Very attractive, green slightly flattened heads have red and burgundy markings on savoyed outer leaves. The flavor of this exceptionally hardy variety is excellent.
AbuLife, Bountiful, DeepDiv, JLH, Territorial

CARDOONS
Cynara cardunculus

A celery-like perennial plant from the artichoke family, cardoons are very striking, with long-toothed silvery-gray leaves, and beautiful artichoke-like flower heads. Found wild in Southern Europe and North Africa, they were very popular in 15th and 16th century England, and their popularity has recently been revived as they make extremely striking edible landscape specimens.

Cardoons are beautiful plants about 5 feet tall with tender stems and hearts. Stems should be blanched in fall for 2-3 weeks by wrapping cardboard or burlap sacking around the plants. Just before the first hard frost, cut the stems an inch above the ground and mulch well for winter. Eat stems raw or cooked like celery.

Cardoon   **110 days**
Slightly spicy celery-like flavored edible leafstalks, hearts, and roots. They should be wrapped in paper or burlap in early fall and have dirt mounded round them to overwinter. Harvest from early summer on.
AbuLife, Dam, DeepDiv, Goodseeds

CARROTS
Daucus carota

Hailing originally from Afghanistan, the earliest carrots were purple, red, or white; yellow carrots were first recorded in Turkey in the 10th century, and the first orange carrots (containing carotene) were developed in Holland in the 17th century and bred on by the French in the 19th century. Wild carrot, which is white-rooted, is found throughout North America, but the roots have a very tough core and virtually no tender flesh.

Carrots like light sandy loam. You may get reasonable results in any well cultivated soil, but it is difficult to grow long-rooted varieties in heavy soil, though round or stump-rooted varieties may succeed. Clay soils must be loosened and lightened with organic matter, but add humus the fall before sowing, as freshly manured soil encourages forked roots.

Plant carrot seeds as soon as the ground can be worked; seeds take 2-3 weeks to germinate, but germination is speeded up if you soak the seeds overnight before sowing. Do not plant in very wet ground. If conditions fluctuate between moist and dry, carrots will crack. Carrot rust flies can be controlled if you skip spring planting for a year to break the lifecycle by starving a spring generation of rust fly.

Carrots can be mulched and left in the ground to overwinter, or pull them in fall and store them in a box of moistened sand in a root cellar.

Scarlet Nantes / Early Coreless   70 days

Blunt tipped cylindrical roots grow to 7 inches, a bright orange color with almost no core. An old favorite for its sweet flavor and fine grained flesh, this is one of the best for juicing. It keeps well through a long season and can be harvested all winter if covered with a protective mulch.
Abulife, Aurora, JLH, Turtle

Chantenay /
Rouge Demi-Longue de Chantenay   70 days

Extremely flavorsome popular carrots developed in France in the 1830s, they are large, tender, sweet, and bright orange. Consistent yields are produced even in heavier soils, and these are superb for the table, for canning, juicing, freezing, or root cellaring.
AllSterLot, Greenseeds, Halifax, Wood

Oxheart / Guerande   72-80 days

Unusual shaped deep orange roots are short and very thick (6 inches long and about 5 inches diameter), good eaten fresh or stored. These are definitely worth growing for appearance and flavor.
AbuLife, Garden, SESE

Early Scarlet Horn   60 days

This early maturing variety is one of the oldest orange carrots still cultivated. Short blunt roots are well flavored and good for shallow soils.
Landis, OldStur

Parisian Rondo   75 days

Small round roots are only 1–1$\frac{1}{2}$ inches long, orange-red and very tender and sweet. Popular in 19th century France, this is still one of the tastiest carrots around, and easy to grow in most soils.
AbuLife

Long Orange Improved   85 days

A variety of a Dutch carrot grown before 1700. Long tapered roots are scarlet to orange with a lighter interior and distinct core. These are tasty, and excellent for winter storage.
OldStu, SESE

Belgian White   60-75 days

The pure white roots of this old European variety are deliciously mild, quite different from most other varieties, and useful for those people who can't tolerate carotene. Originally used as the best summer horse feed in France in the 1800s, Belgian White is extremely productive, but plants are not hardy, so dig your carrots up before frost.
AbuLife, Nichols

Long Red Surrey   70 days

Long tapering roots, often a foot long, are orange with a distinctive yellow core. High yielding and tasty, this variety will overwinter if mulched to protect the leaves. The long roots mean that it is comparatively drought-tolerant in sandy soils.
AbuLife, Bountiful

Danvers   65-75 days

A good variety for fall eating and winter storage. Orange-red roots are 7-7$\frac{1}{2}$ inches long, 2$\frac{1}{2}$ inches across, tapering to a blunt end. In 1927 a major US seed merchant offered an ounce of seed for a dime, and a pound for a dollar!
FedCo, Goodseeds, Territorial

CAULIFLOWERS
Brassica oleracea var *botrytis*

It is believed that the earliest forms of cauliflower were cultivated about 2000 years ago in Eastern Mediterranean areas, arriving in southern Europe in the 14th century, and then adapted and popularized in the cooler climates of mid/Northern Europe, where it has been popular since the 15th century. Cauliflower was little eaten in North America before the 19th century.

Described by Mark Twain as 'nothing but cabbage with a college education', cauliflower is almost identical to broccoli except it develops no smaller heads or side shoots when the head has been harvested. Both curds and leaves are edible.

Fairly hardy, cauliflower is best sown in summer for a fall or winter crop. It is as very greedy feeder, and curds will not form satisfactorily if the ground is in poor condition, so mix plenty of compost into the soil before transplanting seedlings. Cauliflower grows best in rich moist soil and a cool climate – heads tend to be very small in excessively hot weather.

Available in purple and white varieties, the white varieties tend to turn yellow in persistent sun unless the outer (wrapper) leaves of the plant are tied around the head to shade it.

Early Snowball   **60 days**
An old standard variety since 1888, with pure white solid medium-sized heads. Short compact plants do best in mild climates, or as a fall crop in short-season areas. This variety is highly recommended for the Mid-Atlantic regions.
AllSterLot, Gourmet, JLH

Purple Cape   **85 days**
Rich purple heads have a very good flavor and look attractive. Well known in Northern Europe, this variety can be overwintered with protection in most climates. Plant out in fall and harvest late winter or early spring.
Bountiful, DeepDiv, Territorial

Early Purple Sicilian   **85 days**
Similar to purple broccoli; this variety is best adapted to the Californian climate as it originates from Mediterranean Italy. A very tender variety with excellent flavor if grown in suitably sunny conditions.
AbuLife

Veitch's Autumn Giant   **100 days**
A large and vigorous old European cauliflower with very firm white heads. Excellently-flavored, this variety is only semi-hardy, best grown for a late fall crop.
JLH

Early Purple Sicilian   **110 days**
Grown in Europe for centuries, this looks similar to purple sprouting broccoli, producing attractive small purple heads with delicate flavor. It needs more warmth than broccoli; sow in late summer to overwinter with protection in milder areas.
AbuLife

CELERY & CELERIAC (ROOT CELERY)
Apium graveolens vars *dulce* & *rapaceum*

Wild celery is native to Asia and much of Europe, flourishing in damp marshy areas. It was used as a medicinal plant throughout these areas from earliest recorded times but was apparently ignored as a vegetable until the 16th century, when the Italians and French developed thick stalked celery, *Apium graveolens* var *dulce,* for the table. Celeriac, the swollen rootstock *Apium graveolens* var *rapaceum*, was introduced to Europe from Alexandria in the 18th century, and from there spread to North America, but it has never gained much popularity. It is definitely worth growing for a very flavorsome winter vegetable, particularly good in soups and stews, or mashed with potatoes.

Moisture-loving, cool-season biennials, celeries thrive in muck soils and well drained soils high in organic matter. They don't like heat, nor temperature extremes. Sow celery seed indoors 10-12 weeks before transplanting, keeping the seedlings above 55°F (15°C). Keep plants moist and well mulched throughout the growing season.

The traditional way to plant celery is to dig trenches, set plants in the bottom and pile soil up around the plants as they grow, but this is not strictly necessary and you can plant celery in normal beds, just heaping the soil around the plants in the early fall to blanch the stalks and protect them against frost. Some people do not bother to blanch the stalks, growing a stronger tasting darker celery. If plants are exposed to persistent low night temperatures – below 50°F, (13°C) – for more than 10 days they will go to seed.

Celeriac grows in similar conditions, but while celery can stay in the ground until after the first frost, celeriac must be harvested in the fall and stored in a box of moistened sand in the root cellar (like carrots). In coldest areas celery should be dug up and stored in a cool moist root cellar, removing rotten outer stalks during the winter. Replant in the spring if you are growing celery or celeriac for seed, but be aware that cross-pollination can occur between all varieties.

CELERY

Apium graveolens var *dulce*

French Dinant / Chinese Celery   **130 days**
This unique gourmet cutting variety forms dense clumps of narrow delicate-flavored stalks. Resistant to lighter frosts, this can be dried for use as a flavoring through the winter.
AbuLife, Nichols, Seedschange

Giant Pink   **100 days from seed**
This old-fashioned British variety produces sturdy plants with crisp pink-tinged stalks. It has a strong flavor, even when immature. In really hot areas sow seed in early spring or mid–late summer.
Aimers

Red Stalk   **120 days from seed**
The red stalks of this European variety keep their color when cooked, and this 2 foot tall plant gives high yields of spicy celery seed.
DeepDiv, Seedschange

Golden Self-Blanching   **100 days from seed**

A tender old celery from France, with a delicate flavor. This disease-resistant variety is easy to grow from seed, producing compact celery with thick, tender, stringless stalks, blanching to yellow, and good thick hearts.
Bountiful, DeepDiv, Nichols, Verbean

Celeriac

....

Apium graveolens var *rapaceum*

Giant Prague   **110-120 days**

These thick white globe-shaped roots are great for gardeners and cooks as they are easy to grow and have few side roots, making them easy to clean and peel. This is probably the best celeriac variety available, with a distinctive nutty flavor and superb texture, even after long storage.
Alberta, Dam, Comstock, Gourmet

Chicory / Witloof chicory / Raddichio / Endives & Escarole
Cicorium intybus & *Cicorium endivia*

Chicory has been considered a salad essential, as well as an ingredient in coffee, for over a century in continental Europe, but has only recently become popular in the United States. Known as radicchio in Italy, where they are extremely popular, chicories have become an important ingredient in popular mesclun mixes, where a variety of tender salad leaves and herbs are served together.

Chicories grow best in moist well drained soil in a sunny position, in a cooler climate. There are distinct types, forcing or heading varieties (endives, radicchio, Belgian endive and Witloof chicory), and spring or cutting chicory (escarole). Although they are grown and harvested in different ways, their uses are similar – the crisp slightly bitter leaves add flavor and bite to salads, and can be braised or boiled. Endives are often also known simply as chicory, and endives and chicories will cross-pollinate – if you want to save seed you need to separate varieties by at least 500 yards.

Spring or cutting types of chicory should be sown in late spring onward and treated like cut-and-come-again lettuce. Some varieties are known as Italian dandelion because the leaves look very similar; they can be cut throughout the growing season.

Forcing varieties should be grown over the hot season, then cut back to within 1 inch of the root crown about 3 weeks before the first frost, when they will regrow. Radicchio then produces beautiful red and white heads which are used for winter salads. In colder areas you need to force it indoors like Witloof chicory, but heads will be paler than those grown outside. Witloof must be cut back in fall, lifted, and stored in boxes of moistened sand in a damp, dark place. Small cylindrical heads will then appear as second growth; these are known in France as *chicons*, or *barbes de capuchin* (monks' beards). You can continue to force growth during the winter by trimming the roots to 8–10 inches, then stand them upright neck to neck in boxes of moistened sand, and move them into a warm dark place – up to 65° F (18°C), watering regularly to keep the humidity high. Harvest when sprouts are 4–6 in high by cutting them just above the crown. Most varieties will keep growing to give several crops through winter.

Witloof Chicory / Belgian Endive / Large Brussels / White Endive   60-160 days

Discovered in Belgium in the mid 1800s, this is the variety traditionally used in Northern Europe to force tender new growth in winter storage. Plants grow to 18 inches tall in season with long green leaves and tight hearts. Harvest the inner leaves and hearts for salads before digging up roots for forcing, when the second growth will be pale and delicately flavored.
Ledden, Ontario, SESE

Sugar Loaf / Sugar Loaf Large Leaved   60-75 days

A striking white cutting chicory for summer or fall planting. Mature outer green leaves are frilly-edged and lettuce like, while the heart is sweet and mild-flavored. This chicory is an essential salad ingredient for French and Italian cooks.
Bountiful, Cooks, SeedsBlum

Italian Dandelion / Catalogna / Asparagus Chicory   52-85 days

A fast-growing cutting variety with leaves that look like those of dandelions. Sow seed in summer for greens the following spring. The thick shoots and tender young leaves can be eaten in salads, but are best lightly steamed, tasting very similar to asparagus.
JLH, SESE, Synergy, Verbean

Red Verona / Radicchio   65-85 days

Use as cutting or forcing chicory: round tight heads of magenta-red leaves with white ribs are formed in early winter after the first green leaves are cut back in fall. Add sparingly to salads (it has a sharp tangy flavor) or brush with oil and grill. If you cut **Radicchio** back in fall, second growth produces fine heads with a very solid red and white heart.
AbuLife, Bountiful, Cooks, JLH

Bianca di Milano   75 days

An old Italian salad variety, a mild white chicory with a sweet taste and crunchy texture. It is highly productive and copes with light frost. Firm cylindrical heads are dark green with white hearts. Sow in May for fall and winter cropping.
Territorial

Large Rooted / Coffee Chicory

Grown for the large roots which are dried, roasted, and ground for a coffee substitute or additive. Vitamin-rich leaves are delicious for flavoring soups and salads.
DeepDiv, JLH

Green Curled Endive / Giant Fringed Oyster / Ruffec   75-100 days

A traditional European variety, finely cut dark green leaves curl over creamy-white leafy hearts with green mid-ribs. Force, or cut as an attractive fall salad green.
AllSterLot, Dominion, Rohrer

CORN
Zea mays

Native Americans used to sing to their corn to help it to grow better and stronger. They believed that the corn remembered the song from year to year and responded to it.

Corn, beans, and squash were the revered Three Sisters of Native American agriculture. Intermixed in gardens, the Three Sisters protected and upheld each other, supplying a balanced mix of carbohydrates, fats, and vegetable proteins in one of the healthiest early agricultural diets. American Indian corns were the genetic base for all corns, and cultivation of corn sustained the Aztec, Maya, Inca, and other civilizations.

Indian corns are seldom grown in gardens today, but they are the most diverse, developing directly from the original progenitor of corn, Teosinte. Many Hopi corns are multicolored and were used for ceremonial and medicinal purposes, in sacred rituals, and for ornament. They can be used for dried corn or flour, but are most often used today as decorations. Hopi blue flour corn is often seen as the archetypal grain for North America. Precursors of Hopi strains have been raised since about 2000BC along the Rio Balsas of Mexico, and for the past 800 years in the Hopi mesas of Northern Arizona, never under mechanized agriculture. In their arid homeland they are planted deep in the sandy soils, and can thrive without irrigation when necessary, but they also grow well in the warmer locations of the maritime Northwest.

Corns nowadays fall into several categories, according to the shape and texture of their kernels. Flour corns have soft floury kernels; they are used for grinding for cornmeal and tortillas, and for hominy. In flint corns the ears are a mix of hard flint and soft floury kernels. When dry, flint corns store well for grinding, and are very resistant to insect damage. Popcorns are a type of flint corn which are used as popping corn and for pinole. Dent corn is used for tortillas, and for animal feed and corn beer. Mature kernels are dented as hearts are floury but sides are flint.

Unlike other corns, sweetcorn kernels do not convert their sugar into starch. Kernels only color when the corn is past the milky stage. Although varieties of sweetcorn are the only corns usually grown by gardeners, other types of corn can also be picked young and eaten as sweetcorn, or dried and ground for the best cornmeal or flour. If you are not familiar with the taste of traditional corn, eat heirloom sweetcorns soon after picking – they do not have the sugar enhancer gene or others that give modern hybrids their ability to sweeten in storage.

Plant seeds in well drained soil, just after the last frost. To produce reliably, corn needs rich soil and moisture. Drought stress, high winds, heat, and low humidity can all reduce pollination. As corn is wind-pollinated, it crosses easily with other varieties, so if you are saving seed, you need to bag the heads and pollinate by hand, stagger planting times, or plant different varieties about 400 yards apart.

Also, beware raccoons, they will love your corn above all else in your garden!

SWEETCORN

Golden Bantam   **75 days**

This is the standard yellow sweetcorn for home gardeners, a favorite variety since the beginning of the century. Plump sweet golden kernels form on 7 inch ears, on plants which grow to 6 foot tall.
AbuLife, Filaree, JLH, Ledden

Mandan Red

This variety is best roasted. Plants are very short, with up to six 6 inch ears per plant. Mandan Red is a pre-Columbian landrace which has been preserved by the Mandan Indians. It grows better in cooler climates than most corns.
DeepDiv, JLH, Seedschange

Hooker's Sweet / Indian   **75-100 days**

First grown by Ira Hooker in the1920s in Washington, 5 foot tall plants produce very fine tasting white sweetcorn whose 5-7 inch ears mature blue-black.
AbuLife, SOregon, Territorial

Black Aztec / Black Mexican /
Mexican Sweet / Black Iroquois   **75 days**

This extremely hardy corn dates to pre-Columbian times. It starts out snowy-white, ripens to purple, then blackish-blue. It can be eaten as a fresh sweetcorn at the white stage, but is most often dried to produce a sweet blue-green corn meal.
AbuLife, DeepDiv, SandHill, SESE, Shumway

Country Gentleman   **85-100 days**

Introduced in 1890, this 'shoepeg' corn is unusual as the kernels do not grow in rows, but appear all over the cob. Flavor is excellent, appearance interesting, but it is not very drought-resistant.
FloMo, Fox, SandHill

Whipples White   **85 days**

6 foot tall plants bear very fat 7-9 inch ears, each with 14 rows of deep-grained white kernels. This variety has a delicious flavor when picked young, but toughens if it is left on the plant too long before harvesting.
SandHill

Howling Mob   **90 days**

This sweet and prolific 6 inch white variety was named by the breeder, CD Keller, after a trip to the market at the turn of the century. His wagon was immediately surrounded by enthusiastic buyers clamoring to buy!
DeepDiv, Fox

POPCORN

Lady Finger   **100 days**

An Amish heirloom renowned for its flavor and tenderness. Slender ears are mainly yellow but with some red and purple kernels.
JLH

Bearpaw   **95 days**

An old New England variety, the white-seeded silk end is slightly flattened like a bear's paw. This adaptable corn grows successfully at cooler maritime sites as well as in hot arid zones.
AbuLife, Prairie

Pennsylvania Dutch Butter Flavor   **105 days**

Pennsylvania Dutch heirloom from the late 1800s. The 4 -6 inch ears bear small cream-colored kernels.
Landreth

Strawberry Popcorn   **80-115 days**

4 foot plants bear several tiny strawberry shaped ears which have small dark crimson kernels. This is a highly ornamental variety, great for the edible landscape, and for drying, as well as for popping.
AbuLife, FloMo, JLH, Redwood

FLINT, DENT & FLOUR CORNS

Louis Miller Dent   95 days
Texas adapted plants produce 2 to 3 large multi-colored blue, yellow, and red ears. Eat on the cob at milk stage, or leave on the plant to dry for corn meal or for winter decoration.
Corns

Nothstine Dent   100 days
Although yields are not high, this excellent quality corn produces reliably in cooler climates and dries on the plant to provide sweet meal and flour.
Corns, Johnnys

Reid's Yellow Dent   85-110 days
This is the most popular open-pollinated corn grown in the US, originated by Robert Reid of Illinois in 1847 and improved by his son James L Reid between 1870 and 1900. Plants crop productively with small dark red cobs containing closely spaced kernels.
Goodseeds, Landreth

Isleta Blue
Large old-fashioned blue-kerneled ears from the Isleta pueblo in Northern New Mexico are good for making corn meal or for using as autumn decorations. They are best suited for spring planting in cool desert areas.
Native

CUCUMBERS
Cucumis sativus

At least 3000 years ago cucumbers were taken from their place of origin, Northern India, into China. They were enjoyed by ancient Greeks and Romans, and were apparently introduced to the New World by the first European explorers. Cucumbers are said to grow best according to the virility of the planter – but this is probably more to do with their shape than any botanical reality!

Cucumbers fruit in the warm summer months, and thrive in rich, well drained soil. They need moisture in the early seedling and fruiting stages. Susceptible to various diseases and pests, many factors affect their tolerance, with wide regional differences. Powdery mildew and common mildew are typical problems: powdery mildew occurs during hot dry spells and downy mildew during wet cool spells near the end of the growing season. Mosaic virus causes yellow and green mottling of the leaves and reduces plant vigor. Wilt can also be a problem, so choose resistant or tolerant varieties and practice good sanitation and crop rotation. Control cucumber beetles with pyrethrum or rotenone.

White Wonder   45-60 days
An old Southern heirloom; plump ivory-white fruits with black spines are oval, growing to about 9 inches. The flesh is creamy white, crisp, firm, and mild-tasting. Many consider this the best slicing cucumber, but it is also good in pickles. White Wonder is vigorous, productive, and heat-tolerant.
Burgess, Garden, Greenseeds, Landreth

Boothby's Blonde   **60-65 days**

An heirloom from the Boothby family in Maine, short oval fruits have warty creamy-yellow skin surrounding very sweet and delicate flesh. An excellent slicing cucumber, this is one of the very best for cooler climates, but grow it in a sunny spot.
Pinetree, Threshold

Lemon / Lemon Apple   **58-70 days**

Originally from Australia, but cultivated for well over a century in the US, these small lemon-shaped fruits have pale yellow skins and very crisp white flesh. They have a mild crunchy texture and thin skin so you can eat them like an apple, use them in salads, or for pickling. Very productive plants are drought tolerant.
Goodseeds, JLH, SaltSpring, TerrEd

Crystal Apple   **65 days**

Similar to **Lemon**, and sometimes confused with it, this heavy cropping variety originally came from New Zealand. Round, prickly skinned fruits are creamy-white with tender green-white flesh and very mild flavor. Their resistance to drought makes them suitable, like **Lemon**, for climates where others will not grow.
AbuLife, Dominion

Early Russian   **52-58 days**

Taken to Canada by Russian sailors in the 1850s, this early variety is probably the best for short-season areas. Known to be one of the earliest pickling cucumbers on record, it is primarily used for dill pickle but can be used for slicing. Fruits are slender and short ovals, up to 5 inches long, with mid-green skin. Train the vigorous plants on a trellis to produce all season if you keep picking them – the flesh does not get bitter as the season progresses.
AbuLife, Cooks, JLH, SESE

Boston Pickling   **57 days**

A popular and reliable old variety used for pickling since 1880. If you keep picking, plants provide high yields of small dark green uniform fruits all season.
AbuLife, Greenseeds, SESE, Shumway

Long Green / Windermoor Wonder   **70 days**

An old standard white spine variety, **Long Green** has very crisp dark green fruits averaging 10 inches long.
AllSterLot, MacFayden, Ontario

Burpless Muncher   **65 days**

This salad cucumber never gets bitter at any slicing stages. Mosaic-resistant fruits are 7 inches long.
AllSterLot

Cornichon de Bourbonne   **55 days**

If you want to make pickles, choose this old French variety. Primarily used to make gourmet sour cornichon pickles, the fruits should be picked as soon as they are 2–3 inches long.
SeedsWest

West India Gherkin   **60 days**

Cucumis anguria

These were popular in the 19th century, excellent for all sorts of pickles. 2 inch cucumbers with soft spines grow prolifically on small vines.
OldStur

Armenian Yard Long   **50-75 days**

Cucumis melo var *Flexuosus*

This cucurbit is becoming increasingly popular, both for its appearance and because it can be easily digested, even by those who have trouble with standard cucumbers. Very long slender fruits, more like melons than cucumbers, are distinctly ribbed light green, and they often curve into a slight banana shape. Trellis the vines of this heat-loving variety.
AbuLife, JLH

EGGPLANTS

Solanum melongena var *esculentum*

Known as aubergines in Europe, eggplants originate from China and India. They were introduced to Europe by the Arabs in Spain, and they are much more widely used in Eastern and Southern European cookery than in the US. Most people think of them as the large egg-shaped purple fruits available in stores, but there are a whole range of different colors, shapes, and textures of eggplants.

Subtropical or tropical plants, eggplants thrive in hot, humid climates where they produce large amounts of fruits. Start seeds 8-10 weeks before putting out when all danger of frost is past. Eggplants need constant warmth to set the fruit, the warmer the better as fruit won't set at all under 70°F (21°C). To keep the plants producing over a long period, pick the fruits regularly.

Eggplants are more concerned about warmth than soil condition, but practice rotation to prevent wilt and fungal diseases, and don't try and grow eggplants on soil that has previously grown tomatoes, peppers, potatoes or eggplants in the preceding three years. Flea beetles can be a problem on young seedlings; control them with pyrethrum or rotenone, or by planting under cut-off plastic bottles or using a floating row cover.

Early Long Purple — 70 days

A prolific Italian variety, tender and mild, which is shaped rather like a cucumber – only about 1 inch diameter but up to 10 inches long. Fruits have a slightly bulbous blossom end. Harvest these violet-skinned fruits young as skins toughen and flesh may become bitter with age.
Comstock, JLH, SESE

Listada de Gambia — 75 days

A bicolored egg-shaped Italian heirloom, worth growing for taste and ornamental value. Beautiful 5-6 inch long fruits are purple with irregular white stripes and a good flavor. Thin-skinned, they need not be peeled before cooking. These plants are not recommended for northern states, unless grown in full sun under glass, but they do have some drought tolerance, and they set fruit well under high heat.
AbuLife, DeepDiv, SESE

Green Banana / Louisiana Long Green — 100 days from seed

Tall spineless plants withstand light frost and bear light green fruits with creamy-green stripes at the blossom end. Fruits are banana shaped, and should be picked when around 7 inches long.
Glecklers, SESE

Thai Long Green — 80 days

This heirloom from Thailand has light green fruits 1 1/2 inches diameter and 10 inches long, on short plants with deep lavender flowers and green calyces. Very attractive and productive, it is worth trying in cooler areas as it will withstand light frosts.
SESE

Turkish Orange   65-95 days

Originally from Turkey, these small round orange-red fruits found their way to the US via Italy. Tall prolific plants are very susceptible to flea beetle, but resist other pests. Fruits resembling tomatoes mature from green to orange-striped to orange-red, but harvest them before the skins turn completely orange as they then become rather tough and bitter.
AbuLife, DeepDiv, DiGiorgi, SESE

Rosa Bianca   88 days

Gorgeous fruits are white with lavender streaks, very plump with narrow tops and full bottoms. Rosa Bianca has a creamy consistency and delicate flavor, and some growers consider it the best of all. It yields heavily, but needs to be coddled in cooler areas.
FedCo, OrnEd

Violetta di Firenze   60-80 days

Unusual large squat lavender fruits are striped with white. This flavorsome and beautiful variety needs plenty of heat – although you can grow it under cover in cooler areas. The flesh is sweetest and texture best in sunny climates.
Cooks, Pinetree, Verbean

Imperial Black Beauty   75-90 days

Introduced from Europe about 1910, this popular variety yields around 6 deep purple fruits per plant, each up to 3 pounds. They are great flavored, store better than most, and will succeed in slightly cooler regions than most eggplants.
Seedschange, Stokes

FENNEL
Foeniculum vulgare

Although fennel originated in Asia, this self-seeding annual plant has been grown in Southern Europe for at least a thousand years. All varieties grown in the US today come from Italy, where fennel has been popular for many centuries.

Direct-seed fennel in spring into rich well drained garden soil with mature compost – it dislikes fresh manure. Harvest bulbs in fall. They are delicious braised, baked, or boiled, in stews or soups, and raw in salads.

Fino   65-90 days

Introduced from Italy over 100 years ago, vigorous plants form good-sized egg-shaped crunchy bulbs with a sweet, slightly licorice flavor. Bulbs, stems, and leaves are delicious in salads, soups, or baked.
Seedschange, Shepherds

Sweet Florence   65–100 days

Usually treated as an annual, this forms a flat oval bulb which is very firm and white with a sweet celery/anise flavor. In mild areas you can plant this variety through summer for winter production, and use the leaves for flavoring as well as the stalks and bulbs.
AbuLife

GARLIC

Allium sativum var *ophioscordon* & *Allium sativum* var *sativum*

Garlic is believed to have originated in the mountains of Central Asia – Kazakhstan, Uzbekistan, and Turkmenistan. It has been found wild on mountains in Siberia and on the southern slopes of the Urals. Used for millennia in East and West, garlic was portrayed on the Egyptian pyramids: it was part of the food supplied by the authorities to keep the builders healthy, and may also have had a more spiritual or symbolic meaning. In parts of Europe garlic has for centuries been seen as a talisman against witchcraft.

Hardneck garlics, *Allium sativum* var *ophioscordon*, send up a stiff flower stalk that produces topsets, small aerial cloves called bulbils. Remove the flower stalk to encourage the underground bulb to grow, producing a head with a few large cloves in one layer.

Softneck garlics, *Allium sativum* var *sativum*, have developed so they no longer produce topsets, leaving the center of the bulb with a soft braidable neck. They usually produce bulbs with numerous smaller cloves in overlapping layers, and are more productive, more widely adapted, and store better than hardnecks, but they are less hardy.

HARDNECK GARLICS - ROCAMBOLE

Allium sativum var *ophioscordon*

German Red

A gourmet garlic which is very good for northern climates, and moderately tolerant of wet conditions. Introduced by German immigrants to Idaho in the late 1800s, this garlic has a fantastic strong and spicy flavor, but bulbs are not that easy to grow and do not store well. Deep green leafed vigorous plants produce very easy to peel large cream-skinned cloves with a slightly purple cast. The topset bulbils can be planted as seed instead of cloves, but these may take 2 years to mature.
Filaree, Heritage, Nichols, SESE

Spanish Roja / Spanish Red

A popular old garden variety introduced to the US in the late 1800s. Plants have thick blue-green stalks and spreading leaves; large bulbs usually have 6–11 easily peeled cloves. Spanish Red is considered one of the best gourmet garlics, in great demand because of its exceptionally good flavor. Plants need a cold winter so this variety is not recommended for hot climates. It stores well for up to 6 months.
DeepDiv, Goodseeds, Ronniger, SESE

Russian Red

Brought to British Columbia from Russia in the early 1900s, large bulbs are copper-veined and blotched in purple, containing up to 15 strongly flavored brown cloves. The distinctive aftertaste is warm and sweet.
Filaree, Seedschange

Persian Star

A purple stripe variety: the outer bulb wrapper is white but inner wrappers are streaked with purple. Red-tipped cloves have marbled streaks on a creamy background. This old variety has been grown in Uzbekhistan for centuries; its flavor is deliciously mild and spicy, with no aftertaste when eaten raw.
Filaree

Chesnok Red

Another purple stripe variety: very large bulbs have 9 or 10 easy-to-peel aromatic cloves with an excellent lingering flavor – probably the best of all for baking.
Filaree

Romanian Red

Another incomer to British Columbia in the 1850s, brought by Georgian immigrants. Each bulb contains 4 or 5 large cloves, which are streaked red on a buff brown background. They store well, maintaining their hot and pungent taste. This is a very popular garlic among connoisseurs.
Filaree

French Rocambole

An old French variety, with bulbs very similar to **Spanish Roja**, perfectly suited for the Northeast. It has a very clean strong flavor and no hot aftertaste.
Filaree, Gourmet

SOFTNECK GARLICS

Allium sativum var *sativum*

Red Toch

Originally from Tochliavari in the Republic of Georgia, many garlic lovers rate this above all other varieties. Large pink-red streaked cloves have an incomparable flavor, and are particularly good raw with none of the harshness or aftertaste of some other varieties.
Filaree, SESE

Inchelium Red

Discovered growing on the Colville Indian Reservation in Inchelium, Washington State, productive plants have bulbs which reach over 3 inches diameter in good conditions, producing up to 22 cloves in 4–5 layers. Mild lingering flavor sharpens with storage; this garlic is tolerant of most climate ranges.
Filaree, Goodseeds, SESE

Lorz Italian

This Northwest heirloom produces very large flat round bulbs in 4 or 5 layers with up to 19 cloves in all. Cloves are creamy with a subtle pink blush, and taste varies from medium to very hot.
Filaree, SESE

Nootka Rose

Another Northwest heirloom, from the San Juan islands off the Washington coast. Cloves are streaked red on mahogany with solid red clove tips, tending to fade if grown in very rich soil. Large bulbs contain 5 layers of cloves and up to 35 cloves! This strongly-flavored variety stores well and is great for braiding.
Filaree, Heritage

KALE & COLLARDS
Brassica oleracea

Also known as Borecole, kale is an ancient crop from the Mediterranean, known to have been widely grown by Greeks and Romans. It is a non–heading cabbage which still grows wild along much of the European coastline. A cool-weather crop, frost improves the flavor of kale's sweet tender leaves, and in high altitude gardens it is one of the most dependable sources for vitamins and minerals. It is also a good fodder plant for poultry and livestock, and an attractive ornamental plant for an edible landscape.

In the South, sow directly into the ground in late summer or early fall for winter and spring harvest. In cold climates, sow in late spring for fall harvest. Kale likes well drained rich soil best but gives good results in most average garden soils.

Start cutting individual leaves about 65 days after planting and continue harvesting the lower leaves – if they are left on the plant they get tough and stringy.

Collards are a type of kale especially favored in the southern states, where they are a common ingredient in many traditional dishes. Unlike kale, collards thrive in the heat but they can also withstand temperatures as low as 10°F (-12°C).

Russian Red / Ragged Jack   **55-60 days**

Introduced to Canada by Russian traders, this ancient variety has been known in Europe for centuries. Plants have deeply ruffled gray-green leaves with purple veins. In the coldest weather the leaves all turn reddish-purple. The leaves are exceptionally tender, but should be used straight after picking. In milder climates **Ragged Jack** grows year round.
AbuLife, JLH, Nichols, SOregon

Lacinato   **62 days**

An Italian heirloom with very attractive thin dark blue-green leaves. This rather primitive-looking kale is extremely hardy, very tolerant of heat and cold. It is highly ornamental as well as mild-flavored.
AbuLife, Shepherds

Dwarf Siberian   **60-70 days**

Dense crimped and curled blue-green delicately-flavored leaves form on compact 12-15 inch plants. Extremely hardy and productive, the leaves do not yellow even in severe cold.
DiGiorgi, HighAlt

**Vates (Dwarf) Blue Curled Scotch /
Blue Curled Vates**   **50-80 days**

This non-heading type is slow bolting and extremely hardy, and particularly tender after frost. Plants are low growing – around 12 inches tall – with attractive finely curled blue-green leaves which do not yellow from frost or heat.
Greenseeds, HighAlt, Meyer, Rispens

Walking-stick cabbage / Giant Jersey Kale
Brassica oleracea longate
A giant kale or cabbage with a thick trunk reaching
5-7 feet to its head in the first season. The leaves can
be harvested for years, but other varieties are better
for the kitchen. Most kids enjoy growing walking-stick
cabbage, for what is perhaps the best use for this
perennial kale: it can be cut in the fall, dried and
polished to make a walking stick.
JLH

COLLARDS

Georgia / True Southern / Creole   65-80 days
Upright spreading plants produce huge blue-green
crumpled juicy leaves. This is the old standard variety
grown for generations in the South, slow to bolt,
tolerant of heat and cold.
FloMo, SeedsBlum, SESE, Shumway

Green Glaze   75 days
Traditionally known in the South as 'Greasy Collards'
the leaves on these tall upright plants have a bright-
green sheen that gives the surface a greasy look. This
variety is very pest and disease resistant and will grow
even where other brassicas suffer from cabbage worm
and looper.
SESE, Shumway

KOHL RABI
Brassica oleracea var *gongylodes*

In 1554 the botanist Matthiolus spoke of the
kohl rabi as 'having come lately into Italy' so
it is a relative newcomer! Its name derives
from the idea that it is a cross between
cabbage and rape although this is probably not
in fact the case.

A cool weather vegetable, like other brassicas, kohl rabi is fast maturing and relatively
tolerant of soil and conditions, as long as it is
kept moist. As the plant matures, the stem of
the plant swells to a globe shape. Look for
traditional varieties of **White Vienna** and
Purple Vienna, from which all other kohl
rabis have been developed. The flesh is
sweetest and most tender if the plants are
harvested young.

Early White Vienna   55 days
The creamy-white flesh is very sweet and mild, tasting
something like a cross between a cauliflower and a
turnip. Very easy to grow, sow the seed in early
summer; kohl rabi resists many of the predators to
which other brassicas **are** susceptible. A versatile
winter vegetable, even mature stems are good in
stews and soups, or grated in salads.
Fox, Gurneys, Meyer, Nichols

Gigante / Gigante Winter   130 days
This huge Czechoslovakian heirloom usually exceeds
10 pounds, and can get to around 60! Despite its vast
size, the crisp white flesh is tender and mild-flavored,
with no tough or woody fiber. Abundant greens can
be used like kale or collards.
Nichols, SESE

LETTUCES
Lactuca sativa

Lettuces appeared on the royal tables of the Persian kings about 550BC. Earliest cultivated forms probably originated in the Eastern Mediterranean, coming from the wild *Lactuca serriola*. Early lettuces had tall swollen stems and much smaller leaves than those we are most familiar with, although Chinese stem lettuce *Lactuca sativa* var *augustana* is also grown today for its bulbous fleshy stem rather than its leaves. Once thought an aphrodisiac, because of the milky sap its fleshy stem produced, lettuce was grown as a salad vegetable by the Romans, who also recognized its soporific qualities. They apparently grew at least nine varieties (according to Pliny) and popularized a type with a head of erect leaves that they had found on the island of Cos. Hence the cos, or romaine, lettuce.

Lettuce is a cool-weather crop which thrives in the temperature range 60–65°F (16–18°C), and most varieties, if they are properly hardened, can survive temperatures to 20°F (-6°C); cold-adapted varieties will survive much lower temperatures. Seed germinates best if the soil temperature is about 68°F (20°C), but will probably cope with significantly lower temperatures. It is likely to lie dormant if the soil temperature is much warmer. You can plant lettuce in late summer or early fall when temperatures are still quite hot, provided you germinate the seed in a refrigerator before planting out. Keep sowing right through the season, ensuring young plants are well mulched in hot climates to keep the soil cool in summer months.

If you live in an area where nights are consistently below freezing, or where you have frequent rain, a coldframe or cloche can help you produce a good quality crop of lettuce. Open the top of the frame during the day to prevent overheating. Try planting a new combination of your favorite lettuces every ten days so that you can harvest delicious leaves all summer.

Dates indicated are from direct seeding – subtract about 16 days for dates from transplanting. Loose-leaf lettuces are the easiest to grow, as they are tolerant of poor soil conditions, and most climates. Cos lettuces need more fertile soil, but are the most nutritious. Bibb, or butterhead lettuces are a gourmet favorite, combining tight hearts with attractive soft outer leaves. Crisphead lettuces are the most difficult type to grow; they require good soil and reasonably constant cool temperatures to form tight heads, and to avoid bottom rot or tip burn.

One of the oldest of all salad leaves, often classed with lettuce, is corn salad, or Lamb's Lettuce, *Valerianella locusta*. This was once considered little more than a wild forage plant, but most seed suppliers are now offering corn salad which is an ingredient in the popular salad mix, mesclun, currently a favorite in many fashionable restaurants. Mesclun is a colorful mix of salad leaves which typically includes radicchio (endive), oriental greens, arugula, and several different herbs as well as a variety of different colored and shaped lettuce leaves.

HEADING LETTUCES

Grandpa Admires   **45-60 days**
George Admire was a Civil War veteran born in 1822, and in 1977 his granddaughter, 90-year-old Cloe Lowrey, gave this seed to Kent and Diane Whealy. Seed savers everywhere have a lot to thank Cloe for, as her gift helped inspire the Whealys to set up the Seed Savers Exchange, and the rest, as they say, is history... Grandpa Admires is a bronze-tinged leafy lettuce that forms large loose heads; it has a mild fine flavor, is slow to bolt, and stays tender longer than most, even in extreme heat.
AbuLife, Fox, SESE, SSE, TerrEd

Reine des Glaces / Ice Queen   **60-65 days**
A small-headed black-seeded gourmet lettuce from France. Stunningly beautiful leaves are deeply cut, pointed, and lace-fringed; also well flavored, they add a special touch to any salad. The best results are obtained from early spring plantings or when grown in cool season areas.
Cooks, Goodseeds, Gourmet, OrnEd, SESE

Limestone Bibb   **55-60 days**
First offered in Kentucky in 1850, **Limestone** does particularly well in the north. Small compact heads have smooth green leaves and yellow-green hearts. They are crisp and creamy-flavored.
Fox, Nichols

Merveille de Quatre Saisons   **60-70 days**
An unusual French lettuce: the outer leaves are reddish green with cranberry-red tips, and tight hearts are creamy-colored. Although this variety does tend to bolt in hot weather, it holds its good flavor.
AbuLife, Cooks, Gourmet, Greenseeds, Territorial

White Boston   **60 days**
Another variety dating from the middle of the 19th century. The small, crinkled, light green heads grow to 12 inches diameter. They are very tender and slow to bolt, even in hot weather.
Fox, Heirloom

Craquerelle du Midi   **50 days**
A crisp and crunchy open-hearted French lettuce with deep green crisp and crunchy leaves. It is especially suited for continental climates – it grows particularly well in California and Florida.
Cooks, SESE

LOOSE-LEAF LETTUCES

Black Seeded Simpson   **45 days**
One of the most popular and reliable loose-leaf heirlooms. Large light green crinkled leaves have a crisp fresh flavor. Very tolerant of drought, heat, and frost, this lettuce is also slow to bolt.
Cooks, Greenseeds, HighAlt, Johnnys, SESE

**Drunken Woman Fringe-Headed /
Capuccio ubriacona frastigliata**   **65 days**
This tender semi-heading variety is very beautiful, with light to bright green leaves with a red fringe. A delicious lettuce, it is one of the slowest to bolt and is worth growing for taste and appearance as well as the marvellous name.
Redwood

Deer Tongue / Matchless / Rodin   **45-75 days**
Once a common garden variety, this is now regaining popularity. Slightly crinkle-edged sweet and tender triangular green leaves grow in a rosette around a loose head. **Deer Tongue** is very attractive and a reliable producer, tolerant of heat and cold.
Cooks, DeepDiv, FloMo, Nichols, SESE

Oak Leaf   **40-55 days**

Pre-1900 variety, an old favorite with good reason: thick rosettes of deeply lobed medium green leaves stay sweet and tender with no bitterness. Its willingness to withstand heat means you can reap a long harvest throughout the summer.
Dominion, Greenseeds, JLH, Pinetree, Redwood, SESE

Australian Yellow   **54 days**

Light yellow-green leaves grow rapidly to form large crinkled leaves on plants up to 16 inches in diameter. High-yielding and reasonably bolt-resistant, the tender texture and slightly sweet flavor are best from spring sowings. This is extremely popular in Australia.
SeedsBlum, SESE

Forellen Schluss   **55 days**

In 1996, the Seed Savers Exchange grew its entire collection of lettuces. One of the favorites from their spectacular 750 variety grow-out included this fine flavored and extremely attractive speckled lettuce, an heirloom from Austria. It was obtained from Arche Noah, the genetic preservation project in Austria which is similar to SSE. Heads are medium-sized, with soft mid-green leaves speckled with maroon and brown.
SSI

Speckled / Speckled Trout   **70 days**

An ancient German heirloom which has been saved by Mennonite gardeners and is one of the most beautiful lettuces in the Seed Savers Exchange collection. Heads are small and firm, with soft green leaves flecked with maroon. The center is pale yellow.
OrnEd, SSI

ROMAINE / COS LETTUCES

Brune d'Hiver   **53 days**

This French heirloom, a traditional favorite since the 1850s, is halfway between a butterhead and romaine type. It has excellent flavor and color, with green leaves bronzed at the tips. One of the hardiest of all, it is ideal for colder areas.
AbuLife, Cooks, SESE

Cimarron / Little Leprechaun   **65 Days**

A deep red romaine known to have been grown in the 18th century. Tall cylindrical plants are slow to bolt and can be harvested over a long period. Texture and flavor are superb.
Comstock, Fox, HighAlt, Pinetree, SESE

Ballon / Balloon   **65 days**

A very large French romaine with a huge heart. Despite its size, it is very tender and delicious. Good for hotter climates, this variety rarely runs to seed.
Bountiful, Cooks, SeedsBlum

CRISPHEAD LETTUCES

**Tennis Ball / Loo's Tennis Ball /
Bunyard's Tennis Ball**   **55 days**

Best for early spring planting, a variety of this heirloom European lettuce was grown in Thomas Jefferson's garden at Monticello. Small pale rosettes of leaves are flavorsome and tender.
FloMo, Monticello, SESE

Sierra / Sierra Batavian   **55-60 days**

An open-headed crisphead lettuce with good resistance to bottom rot and tip burn. Crisp and juicy, glossy green leaves are veined in red. This variety does not form a tight head until maturity. It is a reliable producer, and slow to bolt.
Greenseeds, Nichols, Pinetree, SESE, Territorial

LEEKS
Allium ampeloprasum

Although leeks were among the earliest *Alliums* to be cultivated, probably grown in ancient Egypt, along with onions and garlic, they have never found huge popularity in the US, even in cool-weather areas. Yet they are extremely hardy, do not take up much room, and are very resistant to disease. Plant from spring into early summer, and harvest leeks through fall and winter. They are delicious in soups and stews, on their own, or in sauces.

Try growing a few extra leeks in your borders as the seed heads are magnificent and look great among flowers, or for decorations.

The Lyon / Prizetaker   **150 days**
A widely adapted English heirloom with long, thick, tender white stems. Growing to about 2 foot long, it retains its mild flavor, and is very hardy.
Aimers, Bountiful, DeepDiv

Carentan / Improved Swiss Giant   **95-110 days**
This old European variety has extremely tender 8 inch white stems, about 2 inches in diameter. Reliable even in freezing conditions (though difficult to harvest when the ground is frozen!) it is very productive and hardy for fall and winter use.
Aurora, Dam, DeepDiv

MELONS
Cucumis melo

Cultivated melons originated in West Africa, but most modern varieties came from Central Asia, an area with fertile soil, warmth, and long hours of sunlight, combined with an ancient culture of irrigation going back many thousands of years. They were probably first introduced to Native Americans by the Spanish at the end of the 15th century, but most of the popular heirloom varieties grown today were brought to the US by immigrants in the 19th century.

Melons like a sunny well drained site, and should only be planted out after any danger of frost is past and the soil has warmed. They like constant soil temperature of 75°F (24°C) or above, and need to be kept moist during the early stages. Once the fruits reach about two-thirds of their final size, stop watering them unless the leaves start to wilt in really dry weather. Lack of water at the final stage improves melons' flavor.

One of the most difficult problems when growing melons is preventing pests and diseases, particularly mildew, fusarium wilt, and sap beetles. Certain areas are most prone to infections so rely on disease-resistant varieties if you know of problems. It can be necessary to control sap beetles with pyrethrum or rotenone to prevent them introducing bacterial wilt.

Green Nutmeg / Early Green Flesh   61-63 days

Very early, sweet, and spicy, this old favorite is good for short season areas. Green-fleshed with a salmon-pink center, it is an early maturing variety, and has been popular in the Northwest since the 1830s.
AbuLife, FedCo, OldStur

Collective Farmwoman   80-85 days

This fine heirloom from the Ukraine is currently available through the SSI Russian collection. Despite its long growing season, it doesn't need such constant hot sun as some varieties, so is good for northern gardens. 6 inch round fruits have pale green, very sweet, juicy firm flesh. Delicious and well worth trying!
SSI

Minnesota Midget   60-75 days

One of the best for northern gardens. 3 foot vines bear large crops of small melons with thick sweet flavorsome gold-yellow flesh. They are resistant to fusarium wilt.
Burgess, DiGiorgi, Pinetree

Kansas   90 days

An old heirloom from Kansas, this hardy orange fleshed muskmelon bears ridged oval-shaped fruits with moderately netted skins. They average 4 pounds and are exceptionally fine flavored with a good texture. Resistant to sap beetles.
SESE

Hale's Best   75-90 days

Heavily netted muskmelon fruits have solid tasty salmon-orange flesh. Resistant to drought and mildew, this variety is a reliable producer of uniformly oval shaped fruits.
AllSterLot, Goodseeds, Gurneys, Ontario, Willhite

Jenny Lind   70-85 days

Dating back to the 1840s, this is the heirloom that everyone always asks for! Flattened turban-shaped 1-3 pound muskmelon fruits are produced prolifically on 5 foot vines. Green-fleshed and very sweet fruits mature mid-season, but the vines do not produce reliably in northern areas.
AbuLife, Greenseeds, Landis, Pinetree

Blenheim Orange   90 days

First introduced to Blenheim Palace in 1881, this canteloupe was a traditional greenhouse favorite for half a century in England. Medium sized salmon-fleshed fruits grow steadily even in cool weather, and this variety is highly productive. Thick, very succulent flesh is sweet and highly perfumed, with a delicate fine-grained texture.
Bountiful, DeepDiv, Seedschange

Large White Prescott   80 days

This French heirloom canteloupe used to be a favorite for market gardeners, but sadly is now rare. Large lumpy melons have pale green-white skin, ribbed and warted, with sweet fragrant orange flesh. It would be good to see these coming back into circulation; they are exceptional quality, and accept some cool weather.
JLH

Hearts of Gold / Hoodoo   75-90 days

Fruits grow to 3 pounds, with thick, fine-grained pinkish-orange flesh with an almost spicy flavor. Plants produce reliably but need sunny conditions and will not tolerate cold nights.
Goodseeds, Heirloom, Meyer, Rohrer

ONIONS
COMMON / GLOBE ONIONS & MULTIPLIER ONIONS
Allium cepa & Allium fistulosum

One creation story tells how onions appeared outside the gates of the Garden of Eden. It is certainly known that the Egyptians were cultivating them 5,000 years ago; they seem to have considered onions sacred, for they appear, with other *Alliums*, on several ancient Egyptian tombs and monuments – or perhaps they were their most important staple food. Onions have been cultivated since prehistoric times; *Allium cepa* have never been found growing wild, so presumably they developed in cultivation although they are closely related to the wild *Allium vavilovii*. Regarded as something of a cure-all since herbal records began, onions have always been important for the health as well as the diet. Red and yellow onions are an important source of quercetin, a natural substance which has been shown to suppress some types of cancers.

Apart from the universally used common or globe onion, other types should also be considered. Multiplier onions *Allium cepa* var *aggregatum* – potato onions or shallots – are hardy productive perennials that produce a cluster of bulbs at ground level from a single planted bulb. Save larger bulbs for eating, store and replant small ones.

Topset onions *Allium cepa* var *proliferum* are also known as Tree onions, or Egyptian onions. They produce several small bulbs below ground level and small sets at the top of the flower stalk. They are easily increased by separating the cluster of sets at the top of the stalk into individual sets which can then be planted from August through November. The bottom bulbs are very strong flavored, but the leaves are good as onion greens in salads even in cold climates.

The best common onions are grown from seed. Sow seeds in spring as soon as the soil can be worked (or in flats indoors before mid-March), and thin to 3 or 4 inches apart at seedling stage. Onions are greedy feeders and require nitrogen, potassium, and phosphorus for good leaf and bulb formation. They are shallow-rooted, and need plenty of water and careful weeding – onions and weeds really do not mix. Harvest onions when the tops have fallen over, leaving them to dry somewhere shady for a couple of weeks before braiding or storing.

All onions prefer a sunny open position and rich fertile soil, with plenty of moisture. Although they are much sweeter when grown in warmer climates, they will grow throughout the world. Different varieties of onions have adapted to specific daylengths and common onions will only form bulbs in appropriate locations. In summer, northern gardens have longer daylength (15-16 hours) than gardens in the south (11-12 hours). It is impossible to grow an unadapted southern variety satisfactorily in a northern zone, so it is particularly important to find out from other growers and seed savers in your area which varieties to choose.

Bunching onions or Welsh onions *Allium fistulosum* are perennial plants grown for their stalks and small bulblets. Plants divide and multiply at the base, but they do not form single large underground bulbs like common onions. Sow seed in early spring or autumn for crops of young shoots six months later, and divide and replant clumps as necessary once the plants are 3–4 years old. Once established, they will produce from early spring throughout the season. They are extremely hardy and evergreen in most areas, with a flavor like strong chives.

COMMON / GLOBE ONIONS

Yellow Sweet Spanish　　　**95-130 days**
Long day. Large 1 pound or more globes are yellow-brown with creamy-white flesh. Excellent flavor, and good storage qualities provided the thick necks have dried well.
DiGiorgi, Dominion, Rohrer, SESE, Willhite

Early Yellow Globe　　　**100 days**
Long day. Most suitable for Mid-Atlantic and Northern regions, this is a standard early variety for muck soils. Firm bulbs of about 3 inches are light yellow flattened globes, moderately pungent and good for storing.
AbuLife, Ontario, Pinetree, SESE

New York Early　　　**98 days**
Long day. Selected and maintained for many years by New York onion growers, this reliable and productive early onion has medium-sized firm yellow bulbs with tender flesh. It keeps well, but its medium pungent flavor also makes it excellent for fresh eating.
JLH, SESE, Stokes, Turtle

**Red Torpedo / Italian Red Torpedo /
Early Red Torpedo**　　　**95-125 days**
Intermediate day. Long spindle-shaped onion has purple-red skin and mild, sweet, pale red flesh. Best eaten fresh, this is terrific for slicing and salads.
Aimers, Filaree, Gurneys, Seedschange

Walla Walla Sweet Yellow　　　**100-125 days**
An early mild Spanish onion with sweet white flesh. Very cold-hardy, this thrives in the Northwest, but does not store well.
AbuLife, Earlys, Filaree, Gourmet, Pinetree

White Portugal / Silverskin　　　**96-150 days**
Short day. Large flattened globes have clear silver-white skin and firm fine grained flesh. Mild and sweet flavor is retained well even after long storage. Good for slicing, and pickling.
Goodseeds, Rohrer, Stokes

Quicksilver Pearl　　　**55 days**
Short day. This perfectly round miniature onion is skinless and thin-necked – a gourmet onion, very early and delicious. Sow seed as for bunching onions to get good yields and even-sized bulbs. Eat these onions fresh and use them for pickling.
Heritage

MULTIPLIER ONIONS

Yellow Potato Onion /Yellow Multiplier / Hill Onion / Mother Onion / Pregnant Onion

Some old-timers grow only this variety because it provides all the onions they'll ever need. Plants form clusters of onions up to 4 inches in diameter which are flavorful but not too strong. Widely adapted for different growing regions, except Florida and Southern Texas, plants can be pulled and used as bunching onions in the spring. Bulbs keep up to 12 months under good conditions.
Kalmia, Ronnigers, SESE

Eveready Multiplier Onions

These onions were grown in Southern Illinois by German farmers in the early 1900s. Pink-skinned and fleshed, they are small, tasty, about 3/4 inch in diameter, and were described in 1943, in the *British Garden Chronicle*, as 'the most valuable, most easily grown, most prolific onion in existence'.
Heritage

Catawissa Onion

An extremely hardy Egyptian onion from Canada which forms a cluster of sets on the stalk tip, and also divides underground to form a sizeable clump. In cool climates it produces a crop in early spring and another in the fall. Not recommended for the Deep South or very hot or arid areas.
Kalmia, Heritage

Moritz Egyptian

This Missouri heirloom has deep maroon colored bulbs with larger than average topsets. It may produce more topsets in the middle of the stalk.
SESE

Tohono O'odham I'itoi's

This prolific multiplier onion was an early introduction by the Spanish. Strong flavored small pink shallots are good even in drought areas, and make a wonderful addition to winter gardens in the low desert. In cooler regions they grow during the summer.
Heritage, Native

Golden Snow Shoe Shallots

This small golden-yellow elongated shallot from Russia is winter hardy, it can be left in the ground year round. Tops die down in the heat of summer and revive in fall.
Heritage

BUNCHING ONIONS / JAPANESE BUNCHING ONIONS

Allium fistulosum

Greely Bunching Onion   60-90 days

A small nesting type onion with a honey-gold skin, brought to Kansas from the East in covered wagons over a century ago. Strongly flavored flesh is yellowish purple, and good raw or cooked.
Heritage

Red Beard   60-90 days

This colorful and unusual Japanese variety has dark red stems with white interiors, and dark green upper leaves. It grows to about 2 1/2 feet tall and is equally good raw and cooked.
JLH, Gourmet, OrnEd

Evergreen White Hardy Bunching   60-120 days

An extremely hardy, slow bolting variety. Resistant to most pests and diseases, this onion needs only occasional division when established. 4–9 inch slender stalks and pale roots make excellent tangy spring salad onions.
AbuLife, Johnnys, JLH, SESE, Turtle

OKRA
Abelmoschus esculentus

Okra comes from Northeast Africa, where it has been part of native cuisine for thousands of years. It came to the US in the 1660s via the slave trade. The name comes from the Ashanti word 'nkruma', and its Cajun name, gumbo, comes from the southern African Bantu word 'ngombo'. It is traditionally used as a thickener for stews and soups, but can be fried and pickled

Okra grows best on fertile soil with lots of added compost, and needs moisture, warmth – above 65°F (18°C) – and a protected site where it can be direct-seeded. Okra will cross-pollinate readily, so if you want to save your seed, only plant one variety, or isolate varieties by at least 500 yards.

Red Okra   **55-65 days**

This variety produces large plants with red-tinged stems, leaves, and pods. Pick pods when they are 3–4 inches long, before they are fully ripe.
AbuLife

Star of David   **55 days**

This old variety produces 5–9 inch pods on unbranched stalks 8-10 foot tall. The leaves are an attractive purple color. Pick the pods small for best flavor and texture, or for pickling.
DeepDiv, SESE, Synergy

ORIENTAL GREENS /MUSTARD GREENS
Brassica juncea/Brassica rapa

Oriental and Mustard greens are native to eastern Asia where they have been cultivated for nearly 3,000 years. *Brassica juncea* (Chinese mustard or Oriental mustard greens) originated from crosses of *B. rapa,* (Chinese cabbage, Oriental cabbage or Oriental greens) and black mustard, *B.nigra. B. juncea* is most diverse in central Asia and the Himalayas, India, Russia and China, where it used to be extensively grown for its oily seed – a century ago, British India exported 1,418 tons of seed! In Russia the oil from *B. juncea* was once used extensively in place of olive oil, and formed an important part of their foreign trade.

Members of the brassica family, these leafy vegetables share cultivation requirements with other family members (see Cabbage, page 110). Mustard likes warm and humid, but not hot, summer weather; and cool but frost-free winters. Direct-seed it in early to mid-spring, in late summer or early fall. Useful cut-and-come-again greens, young mustard leaves make a tangy addition to salads, older leaves are good steamed or stir-fried.

Oriental greens will do well in a cold winter greenhouse for picking all winter long. Varieties which are grown as young greens or small flowering plants, such as pak choi, are the easiest to grow, requiring little attention, and providing excellent tender leafy greens over a long period.

Southern Giant Curled   45 days
An old Southern favorite with large, bright green curly-edged leaves. Flavor is mild but mustardy. Sow this variety late as it is cold tolerant and slow to bolt.
Bountiful, Landreth, Meyer, Rohrer, SESE

Old Fashioned Ragged Edge   42 days
The best mustard for salad greens; long narrow leaves are deeply cut and ruffled. Very popular in the South, it has an excellent flavor, but a tendency to bolt.
SESE

Mizuna   40-60 days
Hardy Japanese non-heading plants produce narrow finely cut leaves on thin white stalks. Their attractive appearance makes them particularly useful for the winter salad bowl. Quick growing, Mizuna regrows like everlasting spinach after cutting, and it is cold resistant and heat resistant if well watered.
Bountiful, Cooks, Kitazawa, Verbean

Chinese Pak Choi / Bok Choy / White Stalk Cabbage / Japanese White   45-60 days
Popular in China since the 5th century, this non-heading leafy cabbage forms bulbous plants with clusters of large pale mid-ribs, and round smooth glossy green leaves. Stalks can be used like celery and the slightly mustardy flavor of the leaves makes it an excellent winter salad or cooking green. It is a very hardy cool-weather plant.
AbuLife, Gourmet, HighAlt, Stokes

Tatsoi / Tah-tsai / Pe tsai   50 days
Vigorous quick-growing Chinese non-heading mustard. Glossy dark green spoon-shaped leaves and crisp tender broad white stalks have a tangy mustard flavor. Exceptionally cold and heat tolerant, **Tatsoi** is particularly good in soups, salads, and stir-fries.
DiGiorgi, FloMo, OrnEd

Choy Sum   45 days
The summer variety of **Tatsoi**, this has dwarf 3–8 inch leaves, and tender white stalks with a pleasant mild mustard flavor. It makes a good addition to summer salads, and withstands drought and heat well.
AbuLife

Giant Red Mustard   45 days
This mustard has delicate burgundy leaves with light green veins, and makes a striking addition to any salad. It is very hardy, pleasantly tangy, and can be picked for months before it bolts.
AbuLife, Territorial

Red Giant   43 days
This is a traditional Japanese mustard, with deep red crinkle-edged leaves which are deep green at the base. Strongly flavored, this is one of the hardiest of the Oriental mustards.
SESE

PARSNIPS
Pastinaca sativa

Cultivated parsnips evolved from wild parsnips from Central Asia and Central and Southern Europe. Forms of wild parsnip are also common in North America, where they were introduced by early colonists. Popular in Europe, particularly in England, for centuries, they were once a staple food used both as a sweetener and a vegetable, but their popularity decreased with the introduction of the potato. They have never really taken off in the US, but are worth growing in cooler climates for their incredibly sweet roots which can freeze solid without losing any of their flavor – in fact many people say parsnips taste better after frost.

Biennials, parsnips grow best in average well worked soil; they tend to get woody, forked, or stunted in heavy or over-rich soils. Direct seed in spring for fall harvest, or in late summer/fall for a spring harvest. To get the best from your crop, dig up some parsnips for immediate use in fall after the first frost, and leave the rest to overwinter, mulched with straw or manure, digging them up in the spring before they start to regrow. If you want to save seed, you need to dig up overwintered roots in the spring and replant them 12 inches apart. Parsnip seed does not remain viable for more than a year.

Hollow Crown / Guernsey / Large Sugar　　　　　**65-135 days**

The favorite old variety, with long smooth white roots up to 15 inches long and sweet white flavorsome flesh. It gives heavy yields in deep beds, and stores well in or out of the ground.
Earlys, Shumway, Verbean

The Student / Sutton's Student　　　**90-120 days**

Try this one for its history alone! Some of the first written records of parsnips describe the plants growing in a Bishop's garden in Cirencester, England, in the 9th century. This variety was selected from wild seedlings at the Royal Agricultural College in Cirencester, so is probably closely related to those earliest strains. Thick tapering roots grow to 20 inches, and are extremely mild and sweet. It is great for baking and soups.
Bountiful, Howe

Cobham Improved Marrow

Described by one seed supplier as the 'coconut of the North', this sweet nutty parsnip is not, strictly speaking, an heirloom, but developed from heirloom varieties. It is excellent in sub-zero temperatures, and has fantastic flavor, great baked or in soups or stews.
Johnnys, Turtle

PEAS
Pisum sativum var *sativum*

Peas are probably the oldest of all cultivated vegetables. Pea seeds have been discovered in ancient settlements throughout Asia and Egypt, through Southern and Central Europe, and even in the ruins of early Troy. They were first domesticated in Europe, then throughout Southern Russia and Central Asia, reaching China at least 2500 years ago.

The idea of eating shelled peas has been around for a comparatively short time. Previously the young green tops of pea plants were eaten fresh, and whole pods were cooked, either fresh or dried. About 300 years ago fresh shelled peas were the latest thing in the French court, as described by a contemporary diarist: 'The subject of peas continues to absorb all others...the anxiety to eat them, the pleasure of having eaten them, and the desire to eat them again... Some ladies, even after having supped... returning to their own homes, at the risk of suffering indigestion, will again eat peas before going to bed. It is both a fashion and a madness.'

Peas fall into several categories – shelling peas, snap peas, sugar peas or snow peas. Shelling peas can be wrinkle-seeded or smooth: wrinkle-seeded varieties tend to be sweeter, and they keep longer on the vine. Sugar or snow peas, or mange-touts, are small tender peas which do not split open as the seeds mature, the pods are eaten whole when seeds are still small. Snap peas are generally modern versions developed from old sugar peas, delicious cooked or off the vine, with sweet edible pods and seeds.

Peas are further divided into tall, semi-dwarf, and dwarf varieties. All tall peas are likely to be heirlooms or traditional varieties, or developed from them, as modern varieties have been bred closer to the ground for easier growing and cropping.

Peas need cool weather, but if you sow into soil that is too cold, or wet, the seeds will rot. Many suppliers suggest inoculating rhizobial bacteria into the soil when planting, which form nodules on the roots of legumes to convert nitrogen from the atmosphere into a form the plants can use. This does give peas – and beans – a head start. For a good supply of fresh peas, sow successively, or extend the season by planting early and late varieties.

Even semi-dwarf varieties need some kind of support; tall varieties need trellising, or staking with some kind of mesh. In limited space, choose tall peas with interesting flowers and pod color and grow them as a feature among flowers.

SHELLING PEAS

Lincoln / Homesteader   **65-70 days**
Semi-dwarf, smooth-seeded. Not as disease-resistant as some of the newer varieties, but worth growing for its unsurpassed flavor. Easy to shell small peas are produced on productive vines up to 30 inches tall. Great for fresh or frozen peas, **Lincoln** will tolerate hot weather, but grows best in the North.
Cooks, Dam, FedCo, Garden, Gurneys

Prince Albert

Tall, wrinkle-seeded. The most popular variety of English pea grown in America during the mid-19th century, grown in England since the 1830s. This variety was grown by Thomas Jefferson in his gardens at Monticello. Sow in January for cropping in May; save some seeds and sow in July to crop in September.
Monticello

Champion of England   70 days

Tall, wrinkle-seeded. Mid season variety with long pods containing 8–10 peas. This old variety of tall pea dates back to the early 1800s. It gives good crops in dry and wet conditions, and even yields reasonably in high heat and humidity or semi-drought.
SSE

Little Marvel / Improved American Wonder / Extra Early Little Marvel   58-64 days

Dwarf, wrinkle-seeded. Vigorous bushy 16 inch plants produce square ended tightly-packed pairs of pods. This old dependable variety is a prolific producer, and resistant to fusarium wilt.
AbuLife, Gurneys, MacFayden, Rohrer, SESE

Tall Telephone / Alderman   68-78 days

Tall, smooth-seeded. The preferred variety of old-time pea growers since 1885, 6 foot vines need trellising. A well flavored late main crop variety with large pods.
Dam, Dominion, Greenseeds, Ledden, Verbean

Blue Pod Capuchiner / Dutch Capucjiner   80-90days

Tall, wrinkle-seeded. This extremely attractive variety has blue pods containing small wrinkled grayish peas. They are usually used dry for soups, but can be picked young and shelled, or grown primarily for ornament. They were developed by Capuchin monks in Europe in the 1500s.
Dam, DeepDiv, FloMo

Thomas Laxton   55-65 days

Semi-dwarf, smooth-seeded. A direct descendant of the original 19th century **Laxton** pea, all-purpose 30 inch vines produce dark-green square-ended pods with large dark peas. Particularly good in maritime areas, these peas are excellent for freezing.
Landreth, Meyer, Ontario, Shumway

Mrs Van's   65-75 days

Tall, smooth-seeded. This tall variety produces sweet, high quality peas that are delicious fresh and frozen. Reintroduced via Seed Savers Exchange Heritage Seed Program, it is a very good variety for northern climates.
SaltSpring, TerrEd

Kelvedon Wonder   75 days

Dwarf, wrinkle-seeded. An old English variety, deep green pods are produced abundantly on dwarf plants, only about 18 inches tall. These peas are very sweet. Sow this variety from early spring for successive cropping through a long season.
Bountiful

Ne Plus Ultra   75 days

Tall, wrinkle-seeded. This old-fashioned variety from the 1840s used to be one of the most popular varieties in the UK. Early to mid-season peas grow on 4 foot vines with white flowers; long rounded pods contain 7 juicy and uniform peas in each. This variety appears to be mildew resistant.
Bountiful, SSE

Sugar Peas / Snow Peas

Sugar Snap   60 days

An ancient class of pea rediscovered only in the last few years, combining the best qualities of edible pod and shelling peas. Very sweet peas grow on 4–6 foot vines, and can withstand light frost.
Goodseeds, Gurneys, Redwood, Shumway

Dwarf Gray Sugar   **60-75 days**

The earliest and smallest edible-podded pea; prolific bushy 24–30 inch vines bear clusters of broad pale green pods at their tips. Sweet and tender, this variety has been popular with gardeners for over 200 years.
JLH, Mellingers, Redwood, Rispens

Golden Sweet   **55-65 days**

A beautiful, ancient, but still extremely rare pea from India with lemon-yellow edible pods. 4–6 foot vines produce beautiful flowers in two shades of purple. The small peas are best eaten as young snow peas, but are also good dried for soup, and the plants are definitely worth growing for their ornamental value.
DeepDiv, SaltSpring, TerrEd

Oregon Giant Sugar Pod   **70 days**

Semi-dwarf. Large flat succulent pods are filled with sweet semi-wrinkled seeds, growing on bushy plants up to 36 inches tall. This variety is resistant to mosaic viruses and powdery mildew.
AbuLife, DeepDiv, TerrEd

Schweizer Riesen   **65 days**

Large, tender, tasty snow peas grow on purple-flowered tall vines with purple leaf stipules. The peas are so sweet that dried pods have a sticky sweet syrup inside! This pea is a favorite Swiss heirloom, perfect for cooler areas.
Turtle

Amish Heirloom   **60-70 days**

4–6 foot vines bear a heavy yield of moderately sweet peas in translucent pods. Hardy, early, and fairly drought-resistant, this variety came through Seed Savers Exchange from 'an Amish man in Lancaster County, PA, grown by him long before new popular snap peas were on the market.'
Bountiful

Chinese Snow   **65 days**

This is a beautiful and rare tall pea. It climbs to 9 foot, producing white flowers followed by sweet crunchy pods. Pick before the seeds get plump.
AbuLife, FloMo, Synergy

COW PEAS / SOUTHERN PEAS / FIELD PEAS BLACK-EYE PEAS
Vigna unguiculata

Favorites in the southern states, cowpeas are believed to have been first cultivated in Ethiopia about 4000BC; they thrive in a warm climate, and should be left to dry on the vine before harvesting.

Purple Podded   **65-75 days**

Tall vines bear beautiful lilac flowers and dark purple pods. These peas are one of the most attractive and highly ornamental varieties, although they are not so sweet as some others.
TerrEd

Calico Crowder / Hereford Pea /
Polecat Pea   **80 days**

One of the most flavorsome cowpeas. Dried peas are buff-colored with maroon splashes around the eye. Recommended for the Mid-Atlantic from Virginia southward and westward.
SESE

PEPPERS, CHILES & CAPSICUMS
Capsicum annuum, C. baccatum, C. chinense, C. pubescens, C. frutescens

There are hundreds of different kinds of peppers/chiles in the world, all developed from the wild chiltepin, the original *Capsicum annuum*, native to central America and Mexico. This plant has grown throughout tropical and subtropical America for thousands of years. Peppers featured on pre-Columbian ceramics 7000 years ago, and seeds of peppers have been found in archeological digs of sites dating 2000 years prior to that, suggesting extremely early cultivation. Although hot peppers are becoming very fashionable today, the original wild chiltepin contains up to 10,000 times as much hot chemical as other hot peppers! All peppers have a very high Vitamin A and C content.

It appears that capsicums were eaten in large quantities by the ancient inhabitants of tropical America, and they were a staple part of the diet in Peru hundreds of years ago. One Aztec emperor of Mexico, Emperor Montezuma (*c.*1480-1520) had a favorite dish that was made of fish and chiles, but curiously, peppers did not become popular in North America until a couple of centuries ago. When Columbus discovered peppers growing in the New World he took the fruits back to Spain in 1493, as substitutes for true pepper, *Piper nigrum*, which came from the East Indies. From Spain they spread rapidly eastward, throughout East Africa, India, and the Far East; eventually into North America, and finally through the rest of Europe.

Capsicum annuum is the most important species, which includes sweet and hot peppers. Sweet peppers include thick-walled bell peppers used for salads and stuffing, thin-fleshed frying peppers, and thick-skinned roasting peppers. Hot *C. annuum* peppers include cayenne, paprika, and jalapeño types, as well as hot sweet pickling peppers. The hottest peppers are *C. chinense*, followed by *C. pubescens* and *C. baccatum*. These last type are considered hardier than any *C. annuum*, and small pods are hot and fiery. *C. baccatum* are distinguished by pretty yellow spots at the base of their flower lobes. *C. frutescens* are sometimes called Tabasco peppers, used in making the hot sauce.

Peppers are perennials, but usually grown as annuals in temperate climates. They need heat and sun to flourish. Plant out seedlings well after the danger of the last frost is passed, when the night time soil temperature has warmed to 50°F (10°C). In cooler areas, mulch seedlings heavily to prevent the soil chilling, or cover with a cloche or row cover. They need plenty of moisture during growth – preferably with added foliage fertilizer, but they do not grow well in overly rich soil, which stimulates leaf production at the expense of fruits.

To prevent pests and diseases, rotate pepper crops and leave three years before planting them in the same area where any other member of the *Solanum* family has been growing – potatoes, tomatoes, or eggplants.

N.B. Wear gloves, and take care not to touch your eyes when removing seeds from hot peppers.

Except where indicated otherwise, the following peppers are all Capsicum annuum

SWEET PEPPERS

Sweet Banana / Yellow Sweet Banana / Sweet Hungarian   65-75 days

Probably the most reliable variety of all sweet peppers, this variety produces heavy yields of attractive sweet pointed peppers, to 6 inches long, on 2 foot plants. They are tasty at all stages of ripeness, from pale green, through yellow, orange, and crimson red, but are sweetest at the red stage. Good for salads, frying and freezing, these are a particularly good choice for the mid-Atlantic region.

Fox, Greenseeds, HortEnts, SESE, Willhite

Large Sweet Spanish / Bull Nose / Large Bell / Sweet Mountain   60 days

Introduced in 1759 from India, these large fruits used to be stuffed and pickled, but are delicious in salads and for frying. Four-lobed fruits ripen from green to scarlet, and have sweet thick flesh and slightly hot ribs, but heat depends on growing conditions and only comes through in hotter climates.

AbuLife, Seedschange, SESE

Nardello / Jimmy Nardello's Sweet Frying   80-90 days

An excellent Italian frying pepper introduced by Seed Savers Exchange and now more widely available. Large heavy-cropping plants need to be tied or staked to support masses of long slender fruits up to 9 inches long. Peppers are strong at the green stage and very sweet when red. These are fantastic for pasta sauce.

AbuLife, DeepDiv, SESE, SSI

Golden Summit   65 days

This attractive pepper comes from a very old Yugoslavian heirloom strain. Golden-green fruits turn bright gold then deep red, with sweet thick walls. This is excellent for cooler areas, bearing even when the nights are cool.

Heirloom

Klari Baby Cheese   65 days

This squat pepper is named after the woman who has maintained the heirloom stock in Hungary. Cheese peppers are flattened, white when unripe, with a soft core. Traditionally they are pickled whole after ripening from white to yellow to red. These are delicious straight off the bush.

FedCo

Sweet Chocolate   80 days

The skin of these delicious sweet bell peppers turns from green to a deep chocolate brown, and flesh is a rich maroon. Flavor is slightly spicy, and they are delicious and decorative in salads.

SESE

Sweet Cherry / Red Cherry   70 days

Introduced over a hundred years ago, these tiny fruits, shaped like bonbons, are very sweet and good for pickling, canning, or fresh for snacks and salads. Bushy 20 inch plants bear very heavy yields of highly ornamental 1-1 1/2 inch fruits.

Boones, DeepDiv, HortEnts, Landreth, Ledden

Pimiento   75-80 days

Thick-walled heart shaped fruits have a small seed cavity. They are dark green, ripening to orange-red. Many different pimento type peppers exist, but this is the original.

AbuLife, FedCo, HortEnts, JLH, Shumway

Manda / Yellow Bell   **65-70 days**

This Yugoslavian heirloom has been in cultivation for at least 200 years. A multiple-lobed sweet yellow bell pepper, it is great in salads or stuffed. The peppers appear above the foliage of the compact 2 foot plants, providing a very attractive display.
Fox

Hot Peppers

Anaheim / Long Green Chile   **70-80 days**

Cultivated in New Mexico for more than 300 years, these peppers are pale to medium bright green, with long tapered pods. Their heat ranges from mild to medium. A Californian favorite, the red Anaheim is sweetest, and pods are usually left on the bushy plant until they turn leathery, then dried in the sun to be ground into powder. Green Anaheims are usually roasted and stuffed, or peeled and made into sauces.
AbuLife, Boones, Gourmet, HortEnts, Willhite

Jalapeño   **75-95 days**

Named after the Mexican city Xalapa, these hot peppers are bright green ripening to red. Chipotle chiles, used in southwestern and Mexican cooking, are made from large dried mesquite-smoked red jalapeños. To be productive and sweet flavored, slow-germinating Jalapeño needs a hot humid growing season. It resists potato yellow virus.
Boones, Greenseeds, HortEnts , SESE

Long Red Cayenne   **70-75 days**

Small wrinkled pods are waxy dark green to crimson, curled, twisted, and tapered. Bushy plants grow to 30 inches tall. These small peppers are fiery hot, even when very small, perfect for drying.
Comstock, Meyer, Pinetree

Casados Native   **85 days**

A Spanish heirloom chile which is suitable for high desert areas. Productive plants bear medium to hot chiles up to 5 inches long.
Native

Yellow Romanian / Karlo   **55 days**

This old European heirloom produces sweet and hot peppers about 5 inches long and 2 inches wide at the shoulder. They are particularly good for baking and stuffing, as well as in stews.
Fox, Heirloom

Ordono   **80 days**

An ornamental type of chile producing green, yellow, orange, purple, and red short upright fruits which are hot and edible. From Chihuahua, Mexico, this variety grows successfully in containers.
Native

Czechoslovakian Black   **58 days**

A highly recommended ornamental pepper, medium hot, early, adaptable, attractive, and tasty! Green foliage is veined purple, and lavender flowers are streaked white. 3 foot tall plants bear medium-hot blunt-ended conical fruits, red near the base of the bush and purple-black at the top. Definitely worth trying, wherever you garden.
AbuLife, Seedschange, SESE

Chile de Arbol   **85 days**

These attractive plants have beautiful dark purple foliage with purple stems and white flowers. Green pods slowly turn fully red and mature, and the supplier says 'heat is legendary!'
Weeks

Hungarian Yellow Wax Hot / Hot Banana — 60-85 days
An old Hungarian variety adapted well to the cool north as well as the deep south. Long banana-shaped peppers turn from green through yellow to red. Spicy, medium-hot, they are great fresh, pickled, or canned.
Fox, JLH, SESE, Willhite

Poinsettia — 90 days
Plants grow to 2 foot tall and look like poinsettias, producing numerous 2-3 inch pointed fruits at the top of the stems. The fiery fruit make an attractive display as they turn from green to purple to crimson.
Fox, Weeks

Centennial Rainbow — 100 days
Rather similar to **Poinsettia**, and great planted as neighbors, vigorous bush plants produce a mass of small extremely hot peppers which turn from cream to violet to orange to red.
Fox

Habañero — 95 days
Capsicum chinense
The most powerful pepper in the world, these may have originated in Cuba – Habañero means 'from Havana' in Spanish. Also common in Brazil and the West Indies, **Habañeros** are used in many Caribbean dishes. Small and thin-fleshed, they are slow to germinate, and require a long and hot growing season to yield well, but plants will grow in cooler areas although they will be less productive. J L Hudson, seedsman, recommends '3 **habañeros** in 16 quarts of stew for a hot effect!'
Boones, HortEnts, JLH, SESE, Weeks

Valentine
Capsicum baccatum
Hundreds of small, round, orange to red pods will appear on a single 3 foot plant from South America! This variety is fairly hardy and fruits are extremely hot.
Weeks

Tabasco pepper
Capsicum frutescens
Originally from Mexico, this grows best in the South and East. It looks like a variety of *Capsicum annuum*, but greenish-white flowers grow on upright stalks and fruits point upward. Grow this to make your own strong hot sauces.
Redwood, Shumway, TomGro, Weeks

Rocoto
Capsicum pubescens
This Ecuadorian variety has fuzzy leaves and large purple flowers. Round, yellow or orange, thick-walled and extremely fiery fruits have dark brown seeds. **Rocoto** requires long daylength and a long growing season, but tolerates cool climates and high altitudes. Fruits were prized by the Incas for their unique flavor.
Weeks

Aji Amarillo Mirasol
Capsicum baccatum var *pendulum*
This is a traditional variety, popular throughout the southern Andes, but rarely seen elsewhere. It has been cultivated for almost 4000 years. Shiny, orange-yellow slender tapered peppers grow to about 5 inches long, and are extremely hot.
DeepDiv, Weeks

Aji Colorado Chile — 78-85 days
Capsicum baccatum var *pendulum*
Another traditional old variety, short sprawling Andean shrubs produce brilliantly colored fiery chiles. They are conical, slightly wrinkled, and shiny orange-red.
DeepDiv

POTATOES
Solanum tuberosum

Potatoes are one of the most important food-stuffs in the world. They are also among the most diverse, encompassing a huge range of varieties, some of which have been cultivated for thousands of years. Potatoes originated in the High Andes, in Peru, Columbia, and Bolivia, and were probably domesticated by humans when the Andes were first colonized, about 10,000 years ago. Tuber-bearing species of *Solanum* are found in mountainous regions throughout South America, particularly at high altitudes and in cool shady places. The wild species are much more diverse than the modern cultivated potato, and potatoes owe their great success to their ability to flourish in high areas where corn, wheat, or rice would not grow. From their South American origins, potatoes have spread to the far corners of the world, adapting to short and long daylengths, to warmer and cooler climates. Some varieties widely cultivated in Inca times are still important today. Despite their ancestry, potatoes only came to the Northern States of America with early Irish settlers.

Potatoes are the easiest of all vegetables to grow, provided they receive sufficient water during the growing season, and are protected from frost. They prefer a light sandy soil, but will grow almost anywhere, providing the soil is richly manured to provide ample nitrogen and moisture.

Although potato plants do produce a small amount of seed, they only come true to type if they are reproduced vegetatively – by saving some of the previous year's crop and replanting sprouting tubers. Small seed potatoes can be planted whole, eyes up, 1-3 inches deep. Cut larger tubers into pieces with at least two eyes or sprouts per piece. Cut as you plant, or no more than a few days ahead of planting. Before planting it is advisable to warm and greensprout (chit) the seed, which reduces field time by 10-14 days. Full scale greensprouting takes about a month: warm uncut tubers at 65-70°F (15-21°C) in the dark, exposing them to light as soon as sprouts appear. The light will turn the sprouts green and keep them short and stocky. Rather than greensprouting, you can simply warm the seed for 48-72 hours at 70°F (21°C) to improve germination rate and yield.

Some gardeners like to treat potatoes before planting them by dusting the pieces with a very light coating of sulfur to discourage bacterial infections or scab.

Wherever fall is long and mild - the mid-Atlantic region, Southern Midwest and into the Deep South – plant potatoes late, in July and August, to avoid Colorado Potato Beetle. Otherwise plant in spring, but wait until risk of hard frost is passed and don't plant potatoes when the soil is too cold and wet.

Tuber set roughly coincides with potato blossoming, so it is easy to tell when potatoes are ready for picking. If you want to store potatoes, wait to pick them until plants are fully mature, at least two weeks after the vines have withered and potato skins have thickened. Store in bins, crates, or burlap bags in a dark place at above freezing temperature.

Ozette / Anna Cheeka's Ozette

This ancient heirloom was grown for generations by the Makah People of Northwest Washington State, said to have been brought to them from Peru by Spanish explorers and maintained ever since. Yellow flesh has a pleasant nutty flavor. Potatoes are 2–8 inches long, slender with thin skins, and grow very prolifically. These late season potatoes are especially good for the Pacific Northwest.
Ronniger, Wood

Russian Banana Fingerling

An extremely attractive heirloom gourmet variety which was probably introduced to British Columbia by early Russian settlers. Fingerlings are finger-size tubers with very good flavor and reliable quality. These medium-sized yellow banana shaped fingerlings are waxy with pale yellow flesh. They stay firm when boiled and are great in summer salads, and store well. **Bananas** are scab resistant, and late to mature.
Cooks, Goodseeds, Ronnigers

Mandel / Swedish Peanut Fingerling

A dry golden-fleshed late season variety, grown by Swedish settlers in about 1900. Crescent shaped potatoes are great baked or roasted, they set and store well, and are drought and disease resistant.
Ronniger, Wood

Rose Finn Apple

Medium-sized tubers have a rose-beige skin and very deep yellow flesh with a red blush. Rugged plants give a strong yield of superior tasting waxy potatoes, delicious steamed and in salads. Space 10–12 inches apart, and water well to reduce knobbiness.
Moose, Ronniger, Wood

Kasaan

This unusual heirloom comes from a village on Prince of Wales Island, off Alaska. Rich yellow-skinned tubers are about 6 inches long with numerous deep eyes. Flesh is creamy-colored, firm, and delicious. Try this variety in very cold climate areas.
Ronniger

White Rose

The long flattened tubers of this early white-skinned potato have distinctive deep rose-colored eyes. Introduced to the United States from Central America over a century ago, this potato is excellent for boiling and baking, but does not store well. Grow it as an early potato before the main crop.
Ledgerwood, Ronniger

Cobbler / Irish Cobbler

This smooth, white-skinned early potato is named after an Irish immigrant shoemaker in New York, who developed it from a mixture of traditional seeds. It is a very high yielding and widely adapted flavorsome potato, good for boiling and baking but, like most early varieties, it does not store well.
Goodseeds, Gurneys, Meyer, Wood

Caribe / Purple Caribe

Apparently this variety was once grown widely in New England for export to the Caribbean. Purple-skinned with snow-white flesh, **Caribe** is reliable, productive, and early. Flavor is good, especially for boiling, and tubers are a uniform size with thin, easy-to-peel skins.
Pinetree, Ronniger, Wood

Purple Peruvian   85-100 days

Possibly the best known of all blue or purple potatoes, this has deep blue skin and fine flavored purple flesh. It must be the most eye-catching potato of all, however you serve it. **Purple Peruvian** is more vigorous and disease resistant than other purple varieties.
Goodseeds, Ronniger

Yellow Finnish / Bintje

A very good drought-resistant heirloom from The Netherlands; a late maturing yellow-fleshed variety. Oblong tubers yield heavily and are full of flavor with a good texture. Great for baking, boiling, or steaming.
Goodseeds, Ronniger, SeedsBlum, Wood

Early Ohio

Once the most popular early potato in the MidWest and Ohio, this variety is still grown there by older gardeners, but, sadly,is dying out. **Early Ohio** keeps well, yields productively, and has good flavor and texture for baking, boiling or frying. It is very easy to grow and appears pest and disease-resistant.
Goodseeds, Ronniger

Green Mountain

Originally from Vermont, this widely adapted potato will tolerate almost any soil and climate, as long as it is well watered in hot areas. Mid to late season, it produces high yields of an excellent flavor, and stores well.
Goodseeds, Ledden, Moose, Pinetree, SESE

Kerr's Pink

This was introduced to Ireland from Scotland in 1915, and became the most popular Irish midseason potato. It's quite different from American potatoes, very floury and fine-grained with superb flavor. Great for boiling and mashing.
Ronniger

Russet Burbank / Netted Gem / White Russet   120-140 days

The potato that made Idaho famous! Developed by Luther Burbank, this is a wonderful late crop baking potato. Heavy brown russet skin is well netted, potatoes are oblong with shallow eyes and very white flesh.
Becker, Earlys, FedCo, Garden, Wood

Beauty of Hebron   85 days

This tasty heirloom from Maine was popular around 1900. Early cropping potatoes have buff yellow skin and delicious creamy flesh – this could be the tastiest of all earlies!
Ronnigers

Bliss Triumph

Another early variety, this has a light-red thin skin and white flesh. Around since the 1870s, this one is worth trying for its reliable yields and good flavor steamed and mashed.
Becker, Ronniger

Cow Horn / Cowhorn Purple Fleshed

Shaped like a horn, this late maturing fingerling is an old New Hampshire heirloom. The skin and flesh are dark purple, and color is retained even when cooked. This is a great salad potato for taste and color.
Goodseeds, Ronniger

Early Rose

This pretty and tasty early variety has been grown in Vermont for 150 years. Plants produce high yields of long tubers with white flesh streaked with pink.
Ronniger

RADISHES
Raphanus sativus

The Ancient Greeks esteemed radishes so highly that, when offering oblations to the god Apollo, they presented turnips made from lead, beets from silver, but radishes made from beaten gold. Nowadays in the West radishes are typically seen as rather a frivolous addition to salads, fun for children to grow, and a tasty ingredient for a short season. But in China and Japan they are an important root vegetable, eaten raw, pickled, and cooked. They are known to have been cultivated by the Ancient Egyptians, and given to workers on the Pyramids, along with *Alliums*.

Long, tapering, black-skinned radishes were the first to be cultivated, grown in China 2 ,500 years ago; from there they spread to Japan, then through Central Asia to the Mediterranean areas, and finally to Northern Europe and North America. Although white radishes are mentioned in records from the 16th century onward, round radishes first appeared about 200 years ago, along with red-skinned varieties.

Most Oriental varieties are long and white; known in North America as daikon, they are slow to mature and hardy, and generally eaten cooked and sliced like rutabaga, or in soups. They can grow to over 2 foot long in sandy soils! Varieties with long seed pods are grown for their tangy pods which are pleasantly hot-tasting in salads.

Small salad radishes are easy to grow in light soil with adequate moisture; most can be planted from spring through to fall, sowing small amounts weekly to keep a continuous supply. Daikon needs more care, and should be grown like carrots, in loose friable soil, either planted early in spring for early summer harvest, or sown after the hottest weather for harvest in the fall before hard frosts.

French Breakfast   23 days
This traditional looking rosy scarlet radish has a white tip, and its crisp white flesh is mildly piquant. Cold-hardy, it can be planted from early spring to late fall. The roots and green tops can be pickled or cooked.
AllSterLot, HighAlt, Kitazawa, Meyer, Seedschange

Round Black Spanish   50-80 days
Autumn or winter keeping variety has large black-skinned roots with firm white pungent flesh. Grow this variety primarily for winter storage as it keeps well all winter stored in moist sand.
Bountiful, Meyer, OldStur, SESE

Long Black Spanish   55-70 days
Another excellent winter-storage variety. Cylindrical roots grow to about 8 inches. Black-skinned, crisp white flavorful flesh.
Greenseeds, SESE

Rat's Tail
This edible-podded radish from South Asia was apparently in vogue in the US around the time of the Civil War. Long slender pods are dark purple, and should be picked as soon as they are full-sized, 8–12 inches; if they are left on the plant they tend to be very fibrous and hard. In northern climates these will have to be grown under glass, and they take a long time to mature. They are delicious raw in a salad, and also very good pickled.
Bountiful, Pinetree

White Icicle / Lady's Finger　　　**28-35 days**

A mild flavored white variety with tapering roots up to 5 inches long. Although best harvested small, it stays crisp and mild if left in the ground to grow large. Sow this one from early summer on, as it is heat tolerant, with excellent crisp texture, and good taste.
Nichols, Shumway, SESE

All Seasons / Tokinashi　　　**70-85 days**

Daikon variety with long white roots – to 15 inches. Mild, fine textured flesh is excellent pickled or in stir-fries. Plant in spring or after midsummer heat. Watch out for wireworms.
Bountiful, Nichols, Redwood

RUTABAGAS / SWEDE TURNIPS & TURNIPS
Brassica napus & Brassica rapa

Known in Europe as swedes, rutabagas are an ancient fodder crop, originating in Asia but popular as a table vegetable in Europe since Roman times. Often overlooked, these large roots are a very useful winter vegetable, particularly for cool climates. They withstand most conditions, including poor soil and freezing temperatures, and can be sown in late summer for fall and winter crops.

Turnips were also a widespread fodder crop throughout Northern Europe for centuries, only becoming popular for the table in the 17th century. They grow in similar conditions to rutabaga, but the roots are smaller, usually resembling large white radishes or kohl rabi, and the green tops of many varieties are also tender and edible, providing a good source of winter greens.

Purple Top Yellow　　　**95 days**

The favorite old variety of rutabaga has very sweet and smooth solid yellow flesh. It stores well for several months.
Butterbrooke, Mellingers, Nichols

Golden Ball Turnip　　　**50-70 days**

This turnip tastes more like a rutabaga than a summer turnip and has been grown since the 1850s. Yellow globes are around 4 inches diameter with sweet golden flesh, ideal for mashing.
AbuLife, Dam, Synergy

Gilfeather　　　**85 days**

This unusually sweet and mild turnip is creamy white and egg-shaped. A Vermont heirloom developed by John Gilfeather in the late 1800s, it is usually picked at about 3 inches diameter but grows much larger without losing its delicate flavor. You can leave it in the ground for several months, or store in a root cellar.
Cooks, Landreth, Pinetree, Verbean

SALSIFY & SCORZONERA

Tragopon porrifolius & Scorzonera hispanica

Although unrelated, salsify and scorzonera are rather similar root vegetables, worth growing for the delicious delicate flavors of their roots, tips, and shoots. Cultivated for centuries in Southern Europe and Mediterranean areas, where both plants are still widely used, neither has ever gained widespread popularity elsewhere.

Salsify is a hardy long-season perennial vegetable with a delicious creamy root, narrow leaves, and purple flowers; it grows wild in grassy meadows throughout Southern Europe. Scorzonera has a black-skinned root and broader leaves with yellow flowers. It is sometimes known as Black Salsify. Both plants are easy to grow but slow to produce good-sized roots. Sow in the spring in loose fertile soil, but avoid fresh manure as it encourages the roots to fork.

The standard varieties are centuries old – salsify is very hardy and overwinters well in the ground or in a moist root cellar. Scorzonera is usually harvested in the fall, but can be left in the ground all winter in milder areas. Well mulched plants can withstand frosts, or you can lift the plants and store them in boxes of damp sand in a root cellar.

Salsify and scorzonera are good cooked like parsnips or carrots, and younger ones can be delicious grated raw in salads.

Mammoth Sandwich Island Salsify / Sandwich Island　　　　110-180 days

Dull white roots grow to about 10 inches long, and taper to a point – they look like slender parsnips. Flesh is creamy-white and some people say it tastes rather like oysters. Leave **Sandwich Island** in the ground until after the first frost, as this makes the roots more tender. They can be overwintered in the ground or stored like carrots in sand in the root cellar.
AbuLife, Dominion, FloMo, Meyer, ThoMo, Verbean

Géante Noire de Russe Scorzonera　　　120 days

Very long cylindrical black-skinned roots can grow to 18 inches. This variety is the most prized by European cooks for soups and stews, or baked or creamed. If the roots are too thin or forked to harvest, leave the plants in the ground and you will still get a delicious crop of shoots and flower buds the following spring – they taste like asparagus.
Gourmet

SPINACH

Spinacia oleracea

First cultivated by the Persians in what is now Iran, spinach came from Central and South-west Asia, and wild varieties are widespread throughout Asia, North Africa, and Iran, as well as Europe. Wild members of the *Chenopodiaceae* family, such as Lamb's Ears, are very close relatives. A hardy annual that produces a quick crop over a long season in cool damp weather, spinach plants tend to go to seed quickly in hot dry weather.

There are two main groups of spinach – smooth-seeded, from which most modern varieties derive, and older varieties which are prickly-seeded. Some spinach is smooth-leaved, other varieties have crinkled leaves.

New Zealand spinach or Everlasting spinach, *Tetragona tetragonoides / Tetragona expansa*, is often used as a substitute for spinach; it is perennial and more tolerant of heat and drought. Soak seed before planting to ensure good germination rates. Orach or Mountain spinach, *Atriplex hortensis*, was a very popular vegetable throughout Central and much of N orthern Europe before culti-vated varieties. In the 10th century Charlemagne recommended that it should be planted in every garden. Red, yellow, and green varieties are still worth growing for their abundant and surprisingly tender foliage which is a good color and only becomes bitter with age.

Grow spinach as a cool-weather crop in rich moist soil. Leafy greens are tasty and nutritious, and the young leaves are delicious in salads.

Long-standing Bloomsdale   40-45 days.
One of the most heat tolerant spinaches. This dark green crinkled-leaf variety is an old dependable and productive variety. It is great in mesclun and salads as well as cooked.
AbuLife, Gourmet, Nichols, Pinetree, Shumway, SESE

Norfolk   45-55 days
From Quebec, this hardy strain is recommended for fall sowing. You can cut it all winter long and leaves stay tender and well flavored.
AbuLife, FloMo

Giant Nobel   43-55 days
Very large, smooth, thick dark green leaves grow on big spreading plants. This slow-bolting variety is good for late spring sowing as it will withstand some heat.
JLH, SeedsBlum

Viroflay   50 days
One of the most important varieties, much used for breeding modern hybrids. Similar in appearance to **Giant Nobel**, the large leaves are very low in acid and stay tender however big they get..
Shumway, SESE

SQUASHES & PUMPKINS
Cucurbita spp

One of the Native Americans' Three Sisters, along with corn and beans, squash is one of the oldest staple crops of America. Cultivated since ancient times, the very earliest varieties of squash were small and bitter, and probably used as ornaments rather than food, but even in pre-Colombian culture, at least six types of cucurbits were important food crops.

Squash and pumpkin are usually used as generic terms, referring to many different species and forms of winter and summer squash. (In Australia all squashes are called pumpkins.) Winter squashes and pumpkins mature on the vine, and then develop a hard skin that allows them to be stored for months. Summer squashes are picked when young, they have thin skins and are eaten fresh.

All squashes and pumpkins are easy to grow, requiring only moist well manured soil and sun, and they tend to bear fruit in prolific numbers. There are a vast number of good heirloom squashes and pumpkins; if space is limited choose small bushes or vining varieties, and remember that three or four plants may provide all you need. Grow different varieties from your friends, and swap fruits or seedlings; go for the shapes and colors you prefer as much as flavor, as squashes probably vary less in taste than in appearance.

Direct-seed squash when danger of frost is past, into well manured and free draining moist soil, preferably in a sunny position. When fruits mature, keep picking them to ensure a long plentiful harvest. A very few plants yield enough to keep one family going for weeks!

Cucurbita pepo includes all the popular varieties of summer squash, eaten in the immature stage because few varieties are good keepers. Their mild-flavored flesh is good baked, fried, grilled, stir-fried, or in salads. In the US round orange *C. pepo* squash varieties are usually known as pumpkins. *C. pepo* also includes several varieties of small ornamental gourds.

Cucurbita maxima usually grow large and store well for anything from a few months to a year! *Maxima* tolerate cool temperatures and some varieties are adapted to areas as far north as Southern Canada. Their fine-textured flesh is well flavored, but plants tend to be sensitive to pests.

Cucurbita moschata come from the tropical lowlands of Central and South America, and if night time temperature drops below 60°F (16°C) they will shrivel and rot. Usually orange-fleshed, sweet and fragrant, they are good for pies and cakes as well as eaten as a vegetable – the popular winter crookneck squashes are *moschatas*.

Cucurbita mixta is the group traditionally grown in the South, hailing originally from South America, and they need warmth. Their flesh is usually pale yellow or creamy and rather coarse, and less sweet than other types. They are more tolerant of drought than others, and are often grown for their large flavorful seeds.

SUMMER SQUASHES
....

Cucurbita pepo

Yellow Crookneck   **55 days**

Crooknecks are among the oldest varieties of summer squashes, a type that the Spaniards took back to Europe and made popular there. Yellow bulb-shaped fruit, growing on open bushy plants have a narrow curved neck, and skin gets warty as fruits get larger. Creamy-white flesh is good for steaming and frying, and great grilled.
JLH, Seedschange, SeedsWest, SESE, Turtle

Ronde de Nice   **50-65 days**

An old French heirloom with fantastic flavored light green globes of fruit. The skin is very delicate, so you'll never see these in a store, but they're one of the nicest for home gardeners and cooks – the flesh is custardy smooth and rich. Bushy plants are fast-growing and extremely productive.
Gourmet, SESE

**Early White Bush Scallop /
White Patty Pan**   **55 days**

Another very old variety, grown by Native Americans. Scallop-shaped white-fleshed fruits start green, ripening to white. They are best harvested at about 6 inches in diameter.
JLH, Heirloom, SESE,

Yellow Custard   **90 days**

This old variety was very popular with gardeners at the end of the 19th century. Medium-sized scalloped orange fruits have sweet orange flesh; they are good for baking and great for grilling.
DeepDiv

Bennings Green Tint   **54 days**

Uniform saucer-shaped fruits with heavily scalloped edges grow on tidy bushes. Harvest the fine textured fruits when small – about 3 inches diameter.
AbuLife, Fox, SESE

Black Zucchini   **48 days**

Vigorous bush plants produce dozens and dozens of straight fruits over a long season. Maturing to greenish-black, the flesh of these zucchini is firm and white. If you can keep up with supply, pick zucchini when small, but these stay tasty even when they get quite large.
Heirloom, JLH

Cocozelle / Italian Vegetable Marrow   **59 days**

Long cylindrical zucchini have smooth flesh beneath a green and white striped skin. The 2 foot bushes of this Italian heirloom produce fruits which are delicious picked tiny and eaten whole; otherwise wait until they reach about 7 inches and steam or grill them. They have a pleasantly nutty flavor.
FedCo, Seedschange, SeedsWest

Delicata / Peanut Squash   **95-110 days**

Introduced before 1900, this squash has become very popular. Medium-short vines bear oblong cream-colored squashes with dark green and orange stripes and splashes. The flesh of the 2 pound fruits is firm textured and incredibly sweet. Although a summer squash, **Delicata** can be stored for at least 4 months.
AbuLife, DeepDiv, Gurneys, Seedschange, Stokes

Early Prolific Straightneck   **42-55 days**

A very prolific and hardy bush-type variety, introduced in the 1930s. Fruits are slender and club-shaped, creamy-yellow turning golden when ripe. They are best harvested small. If you only have room in your garden for one squash, try this one, as it will probably provide all the fruit you need.
AllSterLot, Garden, Rohrer, SESE, Verbean

WINTER SQUASHES
....

Cucurbita pepo

Thelma Sanders' Sweet Potato   **95 days**

A family heirloom from Thelma Sanders in Adair County, Missouri. Acorn-shaped fruits grow to about 6 inches long on strong vines, with definite ridges from stem to blossom end. Golden-yellow flesh is thick inside light gold skin, with a delicious delicate flavor. SESE

Table Queen Vine / Table Queen Acorn   80 days

The precursor of this variety was cultivated by the Arikara Indians in North Dakota in the early 1800s. Early maturing, it produces good yields of acorn-shaped fruits to 6 inches long. Green skin surrounds sweet golden flesh. Eat the immature fruits as summer squash.
AbuLife, FedCo, Fox, SESE

Ebony Acorn   **85-100 days**

Another variety believed to have been passed down from the Arikara Indians. Small fruits, about 2 inches long, are shallow ridged and rounded. They have greenish-black skin, and flesh is yellow and very sweet. They can be used as summer or winter squash.
AbuLife, DeepDiv, FedCo, HighAlt

Hundred Pound   **100-120 days**

This old Ukrainian variety is ideal for cooler areas – it still grows vigorously even when it appears to have been killed by frost! Brought to the US by Seed Savers International, the largest fruits reach 40 pounds. They are an attractive light orange with a tinge of pink along the ribs. Tasty, and perfect for carving.
SSI

Cucurbita maxima

Green Hubbard / Hubbard /
True Hubbard   **110 days**

The original variety of all popular "hubbard" squashes, which came to North America from the West Indies in the 18th century. Tough-skinned oblong orange-green fruits weigh 10 to 15 pounds, and golden-yellow flesh is dry and mealy with a fantastic flavor. These store well throughout the winter, keeping their texture and flavor.
AbuLife, DeepDiv, Seedschange, SESE

Queensland Blue   **110 days**

Popularized in Australia, extremely productive bristly vines produce quantities of striking blue-green fruits up to 15 pounds. They store exceptionally well. Flesh is moist and nutty flavored.
AbuLife, FedCo, OrnEd, SeedsBlum, SESE

Buttercup   **100 days**

The tastiest of the turban-shaped squashes, Buttercup has been popular since 1920. Flesh is thick, dry, and delicious. Fruits average 4-5 pounds, and are dark green turban shapes with a smaller button on the blossom end.
Alberta, Comstock, Dam, Heirloom,Pinetree

Turk's Turban   **110 days**

Grow these primarily for ornamental interest, although the flesh is particularly good in soups, but rather insipid otherwise. Small flattened fruits are up to a foot across; when mature, the tough skins are orange with an orange-red, cream, and green 'acorn' top. They really do look like their namesake.
Dominion, Goodseeds, Nichols, Shumway

Cucurbita mixta

Silver Edged

This squash is grown for its spectacular large tasty seeds, which are edged with a thin band of silver. A Mesoamerican landrace, it is the forerunner of many *C. mixta* squash.

Native

Striped Crookneck /
Green-striped Cushaw   **110 days**

Cushaws came from the West Indies before 1700; this bulb-shaped winter squash is a reliable producer and vines are pest and disease resistant. Fruits average 10–12 pounds, and have whitish-green skin with mottled green stripes. Pale yellow flesh is slightly sweet and fibrous. Most often used for baking and pumpkin pies.

Baxter, FloMo, Meyers, Pinetree, SESE

Tennessee Sweet Potato   **100 days**

This Tennessee heirloom from the 1800s has white pear-shaped fruits with light yellow flesh. Squashes average 10–15 pounds, and store well.

DeepDiv, JLH

Cucurbita moschata

Butternut / Waltham Butternut   **80-110 days**

C. moschatas are among the top ten foods for Vitamin A content. This traditional butternut variety comes from very old heirloom stock. Productive plants produce 9–10 inch long buff-colored bottle-shaped fruits with rich orange flesh which is solid and dry, fine-textured, and has an excellent flavor. Reaching about 5 pounds, these store well for up to 6 months. However, they may fail to ripen in northernmost areas.

AbuLife, Fox, Gourmet, SESE

Buff Pie   **80-110 days**

This is a very unusual old variety. Cheesebox shaped buff fruits have dark orange spaghetti-like flesh. Try growing this instead of modern spaghetti squash, its flavor is much more interesting, improving with age. Start seed early in pots in the north.

DeepDiv

PUMPKINS

Cucurbita pepo

Small Sugar / Sugar Pie /
New England Pie   **100 days**

Native American Indians gave the seeds of these pumpkins to the early colonists, who grew them as an essential winter food source; their tough shells make them ideal for winter storage. **Small Sugars** yield productively on tidy bushes and the rich sweet flesh is perfect for baking and canning.

DeepDiv, Dill, Fox, SeedsWest, SESE

Rouge Vif d'Etampes / Cinderella   **95 days**

This French heirloom is classically beautiful, oblate, and deeply ribbed, and a striking orange-red color when fully ripe. Drought tolerant, these pumpkins have very good flavored flesh, and are perfect for carving into Jack o'Lanterns.

FedCo, Seedschange, SeedsWest

SWEET POTATOES
Ipomoea batatas

Sweet potatoes are not related to potatoes. South Sea islanders called these tropical tubers 'battatas', and early European explorers called the potatoes they found in the Andes by the same name, and the names stuck.

Known to have been growing in the West Indies, Africa, and Spain in the 16th century, they were first noted in the US in Virginia before 1650. Sweet potatoes are related to morning glories, native to the tropical lowlands of Central and South America, and widely grown by pre-Inca civilizations. They were also known in Polynesia in the 13th century from where they spread to New Zealand, and into China by the 1500s.

They grow best in warm long-season areas but, with a little additional heat, reasonable sized sweet potatoes can be grown further north. Grow them from slips – rooted sprouts – in warm, loose, well drained soil. This should be hilled around the plants to keep them warm. Sweet potatoes need plenty of moisture during the growing period. Northern gardeners should cover the planting ridge with black plastic for insulation, slitting it to plant slips at 15 inch intervals. Once the vines begin to run, lift them off the ground to prevent them from rooting, as they grow extermely vigorously.

Nancy Hall　　　　　　　　　　**110 days**

These old favorites may not look wonderful, but they taste fantastic and store well. They have light yellow skin, and sweet, waxy, yellow juicy flesh. They are considered the very best for baking.
Allan, Steele

White Yam / White Triumph /Southern Queen / Choker / Poplar Root / White Bunch　　125 days

These unusual-looking sweet potatoes are one of the oldest varieties grown in the US. The tubers are cotton-white skinned, with exceptionally sweet and dry white flesh, and very good flavor.
Fred, Steele

Kumera　　　　　　　　　　　　**110 days**

If you are growing varieties for their history above all else, you should include **Kumera** as it is possible that this variety comes out of the original stock of sweet potatoes brought to New Zealand by Maoris about 600 years ago. Very rough purple-skinned tubers have pinkish white flesh and an old-fashioned taste.
Allan

SWISS CHARD
Beta vulgaris

Sometimes known as 'spinach beet', Swiss chard is grown for its leaves like spinach and its leafstalks, rather than its insignificant roots. Chards are among the easiest and most productive vegetables to grow, in most climates, provided they have sufficient water and a reasonably rich soil. They are natives of Southern Europe, and probably developed from wild beet over 2000 years ago. In about 350BC Aristotle praised a red–stalked chard, and white, yellow, and green forms are all considered to be equally ancient.

The showy leaves and colored midribs of chard make it a superb ornamental plant, as well as delicious food. It can be picked throughout the season, withstanding heat and cold once the plants are mature.

Sow seed in early spring, directly into the ground as soon as the soil can be worked.

Lucullus   **50 days**
This old variety was named after the Roman general, Lucullus, who was renowned for magnificent banquets. It produces well flavored greens prolifically throughout the growing season, and may be encouraged to overwinter if the bases of the plants are mulched. The foliage is pale green and ruffled.
AbuLife, Bountiful, Shumway, SESE, Verbean

Argentata   **55 days**
This vigorous Italian heirloom has silvery white midribs, deep green savoyed leaves, and boasts a delicious delicate flavor. However, it is less hardy than other varieties, and may not thrive in northernmost areas.
OrnEd, Shumway

Dorat   **60 days**
One of the most heat-tolerant of the chards, **Dorat** has very tender pale yellow-green leaves on thick creamy stalks. The stalks are delicious steamed separately and eaten like asparagus.
Gourmet, OrnEd, Territorial

Five Color Silver Beet /
Rainbow Chard   **55-60 days**
When people first see this variety they don't believe it can be an heirloom, as the colors are so vivid they look as though they have been carefully developed in the lab! But colored varieties of chard were grown in ancient times. The fantastic mix of colors – midribs can be red, pink, orange, creamy-silver, and yellow – makes this a perfect ornamental plant. Ribs usually turn shades of green when they are cooked, and ribs and leaves have good flavor.
SSE, SSI, ThoMo

Ruby Red / Rhubarb Chard   **45-60 days**
Admired by Aristotle for its deep red color, tender ruby red stalks resemble rhubarb, and dark green heavily crumpled leaves with dark red veins make this another very ornamental variety. It has the mildest flavor of all chards.
AbuLife, Baxter, Ledden, Pinetree, Verbean

Perpetual Spinach / Spinach Beet   **50-55 days**
Most British gardeners grow this perennial variety, which has small dark green leaves that can be cropped over a long season. It tolerates most weather conditions and almost never bolts. Plants resemble spinach in appearance and taste.
Aimers, Bountiful, Cooks

TOMATOES
Lycopersicon esculentum

If you are going to grow one vegetable in your garden, it is most likely to be a tomato. Easy to grow in even small spaces, tomatoes rank as America's most popular garden crop year after year. They originated in South America, and were domesticated over 2,000 years ago in Mexico and Central America. A number of wild species can still be found on the eastern slopes of the Andes, in Peru, and in parts of Ecuador.

Despite their origins, tomatoes became popular in Europe long before America, and the old Italian name for them 'pomo d'oro' (golden apple) suggests that the earlier domesticated tomatoes were predominantly yellow or orange-skinned. Tomato colors range from yellow through orange, pink and red, with some almost black-skinned and black-seeded varieties. They also vary hugely in size and shape: the first tomatoes were typically quite uneven, and often ribbed rather than smooth.

There are an enormous number of fine heirloom tomatoes available, preserved for centuries by ardent gardeners. The huge diversity has yielded varieties adapted to a wide range of climates, from very cool to tropical areas. Tomatoes need good fertile soil to produce well, but some varieties thrive in marginal soils as long as the plants are well mulched once the soil temperature is high enough to support active root growth. Over-feeding will give large plants with less fruit production. Basil, dill, marigold, and mint make good companions for tomato plants.

Determinate or bush tomatoes (**d**) are very productive, bearing large crops but over a short period. Indeterminate varieties (**i**) are long-vined plants (needing staking) which bear fruit over a longer period. Try growing some determinates for their early and heavy fruit sets, and indeterminates for later fruiting, longer cropping, and (typically) more interesting tastes.

There are so many excellent heirloom tomatoes, it is difficult to pick out just a few varieties, but there is something for everyone in those listed below; most seed suppliers (*see* **Resources**) carry a good range of heirloom tomatoes, and they are among the easiest plants from which to save seed.

All tomatoes are sweetest when grown in full sun, but most varieties will produce a good tasty crop even in cool areas.

SMALL-FRUITED / CHERRY TOMATOES

Green Grape (d)
Although most catalogs refer to this as an heirloom, this is not strictly true: it was developed by crossing the heirloom **Yellow Pear** with the old-fashioned variety **Evergreen**. This very unusual variety produces tiny green fruits on weedy looking untidy bushes. The sweet fruits turn a different shade of green to indicate ripeness, and are incredibly full of flavor. This variety needs continuous sun for fullest sweet ripeness, but will thrive in fairly arid conditions. It is worth trying for its fantastic sweet and tangy flavor.
Fox, OrnEd, SaltSpring, SESE

Old Fashioned Red Cherry /
Small Red Cherry (i)   **75 days**
Large open plants produce smooth cherry-size globes.
These volunteer readily each spring. They are good in
salads, pickles, and preserves.
AllSterLot, SESE, Landreth

Yellow Perfection (i)   **75 days**
Brilliant yellow tomatoes originate from a British
variety at the end of the 1800s. Small cherry-type fruits
are delicious and juicy, and the vines crop prolifically,
thriving in cooler areas.
DeepDiv

Yellow Pear (i)   **70-80 days**
Yellow pear-shaped fruits are very low in acid, and
have pleased gardeners since the late 1800s. Sweet
and juicy, and easy to grow in most conditions, these
fruits would be worth growing for their good color
and shape alone.
Boones, Gourmet, SaltSpring, Seedschange

Broad Ripple Yellow Currant (d)   **70-80 days**
This very prolific bush variety bears tiny yellow sweet
fruits, cropping for many weeks. This variety was discovered earlier this century growing wild in a crack in a
sidewalk in downtown Indianapolis.
Bountiful, SSI

Lollipop (i)   **79 days**
Creamy-yellow colored fruits hang on the plants like
clusters of lollipops, and taste sweet and lemony.
Particularly productive in high temperatures, this
tomato is widely adapted, and resistant to many
foliage diseases.
SESE

Riesentraube (d)   **75 days**
This German heirloom variety has been popular among
US gardeners for half a century. Big bushy plants bear
distinctive red pear-shaped fruits in large clusters of
20-30 fruits per group. The plants require little care,
and still produce prolifically in uncertain sunshine. An
excellent salad tomato, and great for snacks.
Greenseeds, SESE, TomGro

Eva's Purple Ball (i)   **78 days**
Originating from the Black Forest area of Germany in
the early 1800s, this tomato performs well in hot and
humid areas, and is highly resistant to foliar and fruit
diseases. Smooth round fruits are pink/purple, and
crack-resistant. Delicious in salads and sandwiches,
and great for sauces as the skin peels very easily.
SESE, TomGro

PINK & PINK / RED TOMATOES

Brandywine (i)   **75-85 days**
This Amish family heirloom dates back before 1885,
preserved by pioneer grower Ben Quisenbury, from
New England, who maintained hundreds of varieties of
tomatoes from 1910 to the 1960s. When he died aged
95, he passed his legacy to the Seed Savers Exchange.
This was one of his favorites. Reddish-pink, large thin-
skinned fruits grow on potato-leafed vines. Although
the plants are susceptible to disease, the tomatoes are
worth growing for their fantastic flavor, ideal for slices,
salads, and sandwiches.
Boones, Cooks, Greenseeds, SESE, ToTo

Prudens Purple (i)   **65-85 days**
A wonderful heirloom variety, producing good crops of
large uniform dark pink beefsteak-type tomatoes with
excellent flavor. Ideal for northern climates, you can
grow this tomato even without reliable sun.
Johnnys, Pinetree, TerrEd

Cherokee Purple (i)   75-90 days
This Tennessee heirloom tomato originated with the Cherokee Indians. Very productive vines bear lots of dusky rose/purple fruit with brick red interiors. The tomatoes are pleasantly sweet and rich. As they are thin-skinned and soft they do not store well, but they are so tasty you will probably want to eat them straight away off the vine.
Shumways, SESE, TomGro

Anna (i)   70 days
Heirloom seed of this variety was handed down to an Oregon woman through several generations of her family, with the story that it originally came from a Russian immigrant. Large, juicy, pinkish-red heart-shaped tomatoes consistently weigh around 1 pound, and flavor is superb.
TomGro

Pink Brimmer (i)   85 days
This old Virginia variety won Grand Prize for size and quality at the Jamestown Exposition in 1906. Fruits are pinkish purple, large, meaty and often 2^1/$_2$ pounds or more when full grown. One of the best for gardeners wanting large low acid tomatoes with a high sugar content, **Pink Brimmer** is thick-skinned and good for cooking, bottling, or canning. Not recommended for northern areas, where it is late maturing.
Seedschange, SESE

Arkansas Traveler (i)   80-90 days
This pre-1900 southern heirloom variety used to be grown throughout the south from Northwest Arkansas to North Carolina. Prized for its ability to produce flavorful tomatoes under humid, drought, or high heat conditions where many other varieties fail, it is also disease resistant. Medium-sized fruits are pink, irregular shaped, and full of flavor.
Boones, Seedschange, ToTo

Mortgage Lifter /
Radiator Charlie's Mortgage Lifter (i)   80 days
This legendary tomato is worth growing for the tale alone! M.C. Byles (known as 'Radiator Charlie' because of his radiator repair business at the foot of a steep hill on which trucks would often overheat) developed this tomato in the early 1930s while in Logan (WV). Radiator Charlie had no formal education or plant breeding experience, but he crossbred four of the largest tomatoes he could find: **German Johnson**, a traditional beefsteak variety, an Italian and an English tomato. One of the four varieties was planted in the middle of a circle, then he cross-pollinated this plant with pollen from the circle of tomatoes. The next year he selected the best seedlings, planted the best one of all in the center and the rest in a circle around it. This pollination and selection process was repeated for six years, after which Charlie was able to sell plants of this large tasty tomato for $1.00 each (in the 1940s). He allegedly paid off the $6,000 mortgage on his house in 6 years, as gardeners would drive up to 200 miles each spring to buy Charlie's seedling tomatoes.

Mortgage Lifter fruits can reach up to 4 pounds. Plants are highly productive, disease-resistant, and continue to bear fruit until frost. Large, slightly flattened pink-red fruits are meaty and flavorful with few seeds.
FloMo, Greenseeds, SESE, TomGro, ToTo

Garden Peach (i)   75 days
This 100-year-old heirloom has small fruits of about 2 ounces with slightly fuzzy red skin blushed with pink. Prolific, soft-skinned, and juicy when ripe, the flavor is good but the outstanding thing about this tomato is its keeping quality. You can grow it in cooler areas, and even if it doesn't ripen up fully before the frosts, bring fruits inside and store them for several months, and they will continue to ripen slowly without going soft or losing flavor.
FedCo, TomGro

Zapotec / Zapotec Pleated (i)   **85 days**

This traditional variety is believed to be the ancestor of all beefsteak-type tomatoes. It comes from the Zapotec people of Oaxaca, Mexico. Large pink hollow sweet fruits are ruffled, almost as if segmented; they are excellent for stuffing and baking like bell peppers, and have an interesting flavor raw.
AbuLife, DeepDiv, SESE

Oxheart (i)   **80-95 days**

Introduced in 1925, this variety is well adapted to high humidity, producing an abundant crop of deep rosy-pink heart-shaped fruits with excellent sweet flavor.
AbuLife, Boones, Earlys, JLH

Bitchyeh Gertzeh / Bull's Heart (i)   **100 days**

This very old Russian variety is traditionally grown for bragging purposes, and to separate the amateurs from the experts! Plants can grow to 6 foot tall, and large pink oxhearts have been known to weigh up to 3$\frac{1}{2}$ pounds. **Bull's Heart** is difficult to grow, but definitely worth a try if you are feeling adventurous!
SSI, TomGro

Red Tomatoes

Burbank Red Slicing (d)   **70 days**

Luther Burbank developed this excellent productive variety which grows well even under cooler conditions. Good tasting medium-sized red fruits grow on bushes which don't need staking. This variety is very high in free amino acids.
DeepDiv, SeedsBlum, SOregon, SESE

German Johnson (i)   **85 days**

Heirloom tomato from Virginia and North Carolina: plants are very productive and disease-resistant. Red fruits, sometimes tinged pink, are generally about 1 pound each, excellent for slicing or canning.
SeedSuch, SESE, TomGro, ToTo

Abraham Lincoln (i)   **75-90 days**

Introduced in 1923, red, medium-sized fruits tend to be uniform and free of defects. Bronze-green foliage is disease-resistant, and the tomatoes have a distinctive, slightly acidic flavor which appeals to many. This variety will flourish even in rainy and cooler summers.
DownFarm, Fox, TomGro

Costoluto Genovese (d)   **80 days**

An old Italian variety preferring full sun, grown in the US for half a century. Fruits are bright red, flattened globe shapes, soft in texture, very juicy and slightly tart – perfect for juicing. They keep better than most soft-fruited varieties.
Redwood, SESE, TomGro

Russian Apple Tree (i)   **70 days**

This variety has apple-shaped leaves! Introduced from Southern Russia earlier this century, the plants tolerate substantial temperature changes, and produce clusters of 2$\frac{1}{2}$ x 2 inch fruits with a strong rich flavor.
SSI

Stone (i)   **85 days**

A drought-tolerant tomato with good resistance to foliage disease and tomato rot. Introduced by the Livingston family in 1889 as a reliable canner, the fruits are rather acidic, not sweet, but keep very well and are excellent in cooking.
Boones, Fox, Pinetree, ToTo

Silver Fir / Silvery Fir Tree (d)   **60-70 days**

Another unusual-looking plant from Russia! This old variety has finely dissected leaves like carrot tops. Plants produce very heavy crops of 2$\frac{1}{2}$ inch round red fruits on bushy 2 foot plants.
AbuLife, SSI, TomGro

BICOLORED TOMATOES

Big Rainbow (i)   80-102 days
6 foot plants bear large numbers of huge golden fruits
with streaks of red running through the flesh.
Relatively thin-skinned, and weighing up to 2 pounds,
they tend to be susceptible to cracking, and do not
store well, but their appearance and flavor are superb.
Cooks, SESE, TomGro, ToTo

Old German (i)   85 days
This variety came from the Virginia Mennonite
community. Yellow fruits have a red center and usually
weigh over a pound. They have few seeds and do not
yield heartily, but the flavor is fantastic.
SESE

Mr Stripey / Tigerella (i)   80 days
This unusual British heirloom is highly productive,
producing small red fruits with jagged orange stripes.
The flavor is mild, and the fruits are low in acid.
Bountiful, Shumway, ToTo

YELLOW TOMATOES

Hugh's (i)   89 days
An heirloom from Indiana, this pale yellow beefsteak
variety has a good flavor, particularly when grown in
full sun. Grow it for its thirst-quenching qualities, as it
is extremely large and juicy, and reliably productive.
SESE, TomGro

Azoychka (d)   81 days
The seed from this Russian heirloom was collected by
Seed Savers International from an elderly seedsman at
the Bird Market in Moscow. Fruits are slightly tart, pale
yellow, ripening to a darker golden color in hot sun.
Excellent for juicing and slicing.
SSI, TomGro

Goldie / Golden Dixie (i)   85-95 days
Very vigorous indeterminate vines produce large gold-
en slightly flattened globes with a fine mild flavor. This
is an heirloom from the first pioneer gardens which
will fruit prolifically in most climates, and most soils.
Bountiful, FloMo, ToTo, TomGro

DARK-SKINNED TOMATOES

Purple Calabash   90 days
This unusual variety has purplish ruffled fruits, with
bronze or chocolate patches when ripe. It appears to
tolerate extreme drought conditions to produce an
abundant crop of very flavorsome tomatoes.
Considered by many people to be extremely ugly, it
looks like illustrations of tomatoes from 16th century
herbals, but one grower stated that the fruits tasted as
though they 'had been grown in wine... would
probably make the best tomato sauce and stewed
tomatoes in the world.'
AbuLife, DeepDiv, JLH

Black Krim (i)   80-95 days
Dark colored thin-skinned fruits are incredibly juicy,
and grow well under semi-drought conditions. The
taste is enhanced with a slightly smoky saltiness – ideal
for salads. The fruits do not store well, but you will
probably want to eat them almost straight off the vine.
Bountiful, TomGro

Black Sea Man (d)   89 days
An unusual potato-leaf variety with mahogany-brown
3–4 inch fruits with black shoulders. This needs hot
and sunny weather to color up, but if you have the
right climate, try it for its excellent flavor and
interesting appearance.
SSI

WATERMELONS
Citrullus lanatus

First grown in the African tropics, water-melons have been cultivated for at least 4,000 years. They have been grown in central Asia for at least 1,000 years, where some of the most interesting landraces can still be found, particularly in Kazhakstan and Uzbekhistan. Watermelons need hot, preferably humid weather to be at their best, but you can grow them under cover, and some short-season varieties will fruit in cooler climates.

Start seeds off indoors well after any danger of frost, and keep the seedlings moist. Watermelons need plenty of water throughout their growing period, but stop watering them when they are approaching full size, as the flavor is better if they have a period of drought before harvest.

Moon and Stars /
Cherokee Moon and Stars   **95-100 days**
This legendary heirloom from Missouri is incredibly beautiful. The dark green ridged skin of these 20-30 pound fruits is speckled with yellow spots. Leaves are also blotched with yellow, and flesh is bright red. This melon is worth growing in warmer areas for its appearance alone, but it is also one of the sweetest of all watermelons.
AbuLife, Bountiful, Landreth, OrnEd

Amish Moon and Stars   **100 days**
Unlike other **Moon and Stars** varieties, this old Amish heirloom has a smooth rind. Flesh is pinkish-red and outstandingly sweet, brown seeds are speckled cream.
SESE

Black-seeded Ice Cream   **85-100 days**
An heirloom from the Pacific Northwest, round fruit grow to about 10 pounds, pale green rinds are striped in dark green. Thin-skinned and very juicy, this variety stores well and tastes very sweet.
Goodseeds, SESE

Sugar Baby   **78 days**
Ideal where space is limited, numerous small round fruits are produced early, on compact vines. The rind of these sweet, red-fleshed fruits turns greenish black when ripe.
Greenseeds, Gourmet, SESE, Verbean

Golden Jubilee   **90 days**
This yellow-fleshed Florida heirloom needs a long season to produce long oval melons weighing up to 40 pounds. The thick rind is pale green with dark green stripes, and flavor and texture are good.
SESE

Kleckley Sweet / Monte Cristo   **80-90 days**
This has been a favorite garden variety for 150 years. Glossy dark green oblong fruits are thin-skinned with sweet deep red flesh, and huge white seeds. Very reliable in the South, this is a good glasshouse variety for cooler areas.
DownFarm, JLH, Shumway

Tom Watson   **80-95 days**
The best adapted watermelon for Canada and north-ern states of the US. Large fruits – growing to 40 pounds – have sweet dark red flesh.
Landreth, Shumway, Willhite

PART

2

Resources

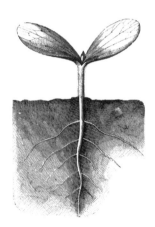

THE DIRECTORY – RESOURCES
SEED SUPPLIERS

While we have done our best to ensure that this information is accurate and up-to-date at the time of publication, from time to time companies change, new individuals start trading, and some others take a break. No list such as this can ever be complete, there are sure to be some others out there providing a wonderful service in saving and supplying seeds as stewards of the future. We apologize for any omissions, and thank all suppliers for their great work. Any prices quoted for catalogs are correct at the time of printing.

Initial entries in bold script relate to suppliers' codes in the Directory

AbuLife
Abundant Life Seed Foundation
PO Box 772
Port Townsend
WA 98368
Tel: (360) 385-5660
Fax: (360) 385-7455

Non-profit corporation which aims to preserve genetic diversity and support sustainable agriculture through acquiring, propagating, and preserving native and naturalized seed, with specific emphasis on those species not commercially available, including rare and endangered species. Established World Seed Fund in 1985 to send seeds to impoverished communities worldwide.
All seeds open-pollinated, many organically grown or wildcrafted.
● Catalog $2.00
see also page 181

Aimers
Aimers Seeds
81 Temperance St
Aurora
Ontario L4G 1R1
Canada

Good range of heirloom vegetable varieties and regional wild flowers.
● Free catalog.

Alberta
Alberta Nurseries and Seeds Ltd
Box 20, Bowden
Alberta
T0M 0K0
Canada
Tel: (403) 224-3544
Fax: (403) 224-2455

Specializes in seeds for short season areas.
● Free catalog.

Allan
Ken Allan – Garden Research Exchange
61 South Bartlett Street
Kingston
Ontario K7K 1X3
Canada

Organically grown vegetable seed species suitable for northern growers. Publishes research by home gardeners on garden vegetables.
◆ Ships seed to US and Canada, sweet potato and potato tubers to US only.
● Free pricelist.

AllSterLot
Allen, Sterling & Lothrop
191 US Route 1
Falmouth
ME 04105-1385
Tel: (207) 781-4142
Fax: (207) 781-4143

Specializes in vegetable seeds adapted to New England climate. Supplies open-pollinated corn seed.
◆ Shipping within US only, excluding Hawaii and Alaska.
● Catalog $1.00 refundable with first order.

The American Gourd Society
PO Box 274
Mount Gilead
OH 43338-0274
Tel/fax: (419) 362-6446

Supplies gourd seeds, gourd books, and paraphernalia!
● Free catalog.

Archias
Archias' Seed Store
106 East Main St
Sedalia
MO 65301-3849
Tel: (816) 826-1330

Founded in 1884, one of the oldest seed houses in the US. Supplies a range of open-pollinated vegetables, flowers, bulbs, and strawberries.
● Catalog $1.00.

Aurora
Aurora Biodynamic Farm
RR1 63-9
Creston
BC V0B 1G0
Canada
Tel/fax: (604) 428-4404
email: http://www.awinc.aurora

Supplies open-pollinated heirloom seeds of vegetables, flowers, and herbs. All seeds are biodynamically cultivated and untreated. Aurora runs a biodynamic agriculture training program.
● Catalog $3.00.
see also page 181

Baxter
Baxter Seed Co
PO Box 8175
Weslaco
TX 785396
Tel: (210) 968-3187

Range includes open-pollinated heirloom vegetable varieties.
● Free pricelist.

Becker
Becker's Seed Potatoes
RR 1
Trout Creek
Ontario
P0H 2L0
Canada
Tel: (705) 724-2305

Good range of traditional, old-fashioned and heirloom potatoes.
◆ Ships to Canada only.
● Free catalog.

Boones
Boone's Native Seed Company
PO Box 10363
Raleigh
NC 27605
Website:
http://www.nando.net/ads/boone-seed

Specializes in heirloom and traditional tomatoes, and chile peppers; open-pollinated seeds of native wildflowers and grasses indigenous to the Americas before European settlement. Most seeds are grown organically or wild-crafted. All seeds are untreated.
● Free catalog, includes information about the history of the plants.

Leonard Borries
RT 4 Box 79
Teutopolis
IL 62467
Tel: (217) 857-3377

Open-pollinated corn, four varieties.
● Free pricelist.

Bountiful
Bountiful Gardens
18001 Shafer Ranch Road
Willits
CA 95490
Tel/fax: (707) 459-6410
website: http://www.olympus.net/gardens/welcome.html

Specializing in heirloom varieties, Bountiful Gardens is a family-run organization supplying over 300 varieties of open-pollinated untreated seeds, organically, bio-intensively or naturally grown. Also supplies range of organically grown seeds from the Henry Doubleday Research Association in England.
◆ Ships seeds abroad.
● Heirloom catalog free.
● Rare seeds catalog $2.00.
● Bulk pricelist $1.00.

Burgess
Burgess Seed and Plant Co
905 Four Seasons Road
Bloomington
IL 61701

Old established firm supplying unique and popular vegetable seeds.
● Catalog $1.00.

Burrell
D V Burrell Seed Growers Co
PO Box 150
Rocky Ford
CO 81067
Tel: (719) 254-3318
Fax: (719) 254-3319

Commercial seed grower, but some untreated and open-pollinated seeds are available.
● Free catalog.

Butterbrooke
Butterbrooke Farm
78 Barry Road
Oxford
CT 06478-1529
Tel: (203) 888-2000

Part of a Network of Organic Growers and Seed Savers, this seed co-operative will sell small amounts to non-members. Supplies many untreated open-pollinated seeds of short maturity heirloom varieties.
● Free pricelist.
see also page 181

Comstock
Comstock, Ferre & Co
253 Main Street
Wethersfield
CT 06109
Tel: (203) 571-6590
Fax: (203) 571-6595

Large catalog of vegetable varieties includes a number of traditional and heirloom open-pollinated varieties; annuals, herbs, and perennials
● Catalog $3.00 refundable with first order.

Cooks
The Cook's Garden
PO Box 535
Londonderry
VT 05148
Tel: (802) 824-3400
Fax: (802) 824-3027

Focuses on vegetables for cooks, especially European salad greens, specialty vegetables, and heirloom varieties from Europe and US. All seeds are untreated.
◆ Ships outside US.
● Free catalog.

Corns
Carl L and Karen D Barnes
RT 1
Box 32
Turpin
OK 73950

Family grown open-pollinated dent corns, flint corns, and popcorns.
● Pricelist $1.00 with SASE.

Cross
Cross Enterprises
109 9th Street
Bunker Hill
KS 67626
Tel: (913) 483-6163
Fax: (913) 483-6240

Organically grown beans, grains, and sprouting seeds.
● Free catalog.

Dam
William Dam Seeds Ltd
Box 8400 Dundas
Ontario L9H 6M1
Canada
Tel: (905) 628-6641

Untreated seeds of European varieties, including many heirlooms.
● Catalog free in Canada, $2.00 in US.

DeepDiv
Deep Diversity
PO Box 15700
1212 Parkway Drive
Santa Fe
NM 87506

see also **Seeds of Change**

The **Deep Diversity** catalog focuses on kinship conservation gardening, emphasizing the link between species and families, the interconnectedness of organisms, the merits of seed saving, and the importance of organic gardening. All seeds in the Deep Diversity catalog are grown organically on the **Seeds of Change** farm, or gathered from the wild where this will not distort a healthy ecosystem. This list includes the seeds of many rare and endangered wild plants.
◆ Ships seed to US, Canada, and Mexico; tubers and bulbs within US only.
● Catalog $4.00 (contains detailed descriptions)
● Seed list $1.00.

DiGiorgi
DiGiorgi Seed Company
6011 North Street
Omaha
NE 68117

List includes a good number of open-pollinated heirloom vegetable varieties.
● Free catalog.

Dill
Howard Dill Enterprises
400 College Road
Windsor
Nova Scotia BON 2TO
Canada
Tel: (902) 798-2728
Fax: (902) 798-0842

Giant pumpkin and squash specialist.
● Free pricelist.

Dominion
Dominion Seed House
Box 2500
Georgetown
Ontario L7G 5L6
Canada

Short-season varieties.
◆ Ships to Canada only.
● Catalog $1.00.

DownFarm
Down on the Farm Seed
PO Box 184
Hiram
OH 44234

Untreated seed of many old-fashioned varieties, mostly open-pollinated.
● Free pricelist.

Earlys
Early's Farm and Garden Centre
2615 Lorne Avenue
Saskatoon
Saskatchewan S7J 0S5
Canada
Tel: (306) 931-1982

Long-established seed merchant, supplying a range of traditional open-pollinated varieties suitable for short-season areas.
● Catalogue $2.00.

ECHO
ECHO Seed Sales
see page 181

Ecogenesis Inc
16 Jedburgh Road
Toronto
Ontario M5M 3J6
Canada

Open-pollinated insect- and disease-resistant vegetable varieties for organic gardeners. All seeds are untreated.
● Catalog $2.00.

Evergreen YH Enterprises
PO Box 17538
Anaheim
CA 92817
Fax: (714) 637-5769

More than 150 varieties of
Oriental vegetable seeds.
● Catalog $2.00.

FedCo
Fedco Seeds & Moose Tubers
PO Box 520
Waterville
ME 04903-0520
Tel: (207) 873-7333

A seed co-operative, growing
many unusual heirloom varieties
and a wide range of vegetables
specially adapted for Northeastern
climates. Some seeds are organically grown, all seeds are untreated, no transgenic cultivars.
◆ Ships throughout US including
Alaska and Hawaii.
● Catalog $1.00.
Moose Tubers specializes in seed
potatoes, onion sets, and
sunchokes.

Field *Receiv* ✓
Henry Field's Seed & Nursery Co
PO Box 700
Shenandoah
IA 51602
Tel: (605) 665-9391
Fax: (605) 665-2601

Century-old company supplies a
range od heirloom vegetables in
its mail order garden seed and
nursery stock.
◆ Ships to the 48 contiguous
United States only.
● Free catalog.

Filaree
Filaree Farm
182 Conconully Highway
Okanogan
WA 98840
Tel: (509) 422-6940 (message only)

The widest selection of garlics in
the US, all organically grown. Not
suitable for latitudes south of
32°N, such as Florida, Southern
Louisiana, Southern Texas, and
Hawaii.
◆ Ships within US.
● Catalog $2.00.

Fish Lake Garlic Man
Ted Mackza
Research and Experimental Station
RR2, Demorestville
Ontario
KOK 1WO
Tel: (613) 476-8030

A non-profit organization, dedicated to making Canada self-sufficient in garlic, and to developing
the finest garlic in the world! A
wide variety of garlics, plus useful
cultivation information. Visitors to
Ted Mackza's research station are
welcome, but call first.
● Price list and information $3.00.
+ SASE in Canada, $3.00 + postal
coupon elsewhere.

FloMo
Floating Mountain Seeds
PO Box 1275
Port Angeles
WA 98362

Organically grown, open-pollinated heirloom vegetables.
● Catalog $2.00.

Freds
Fred's Plant Farm
4589 Ralston Road
Martin
TN 38237
Tel: (800) 550-2575

Collection of sweet potatoes.
● Free pricelist.

Fox
**Fox Hollow Herb and Heirloom
Seed Co**
PO Box 148
McGrann
PA 16236
Tel: (412) 548-SEED

Small family-owned company
committed to perpetuation of
open-pollinated heirloom vegetables, plus herbs and old standard
flowers. Most seed is grown
organically, all seeds untreated
and sorted by hand.
◆ Ships to US, Canada, and
Mexico.
● Catalog $1.00.

Garden
Garden City Seeds
1324 Red Crow Road
Victor
MT 59875
Tel: (406) 961-4837
Fax: (406) 961-4877

Specializes in hardy varieties for
the north. All seeds are untreated,
many organically grown.
● Catalog $1.00.

Giant Watermelons
PO Box 141
Hope
AR 71801

Watermelon and cantaloupe
seeds.
● Catalog free with SASE.

Glecklers
Gleckler's Seedsmen
Metamora
OH 43540

Open-pollinated heirloom and foreign vegetable seeds, plus a large
selection of American Indian
squash.
● Free catalog.

Goodseeds
Good Seed Co
Star Route Box 73A
Oroville (Chesaw)
WA 98844

Specializes in heirloom seeds.
● Catalog $3.00.

Gourmet
The Gourmet Gardener
8650 College Boulevard
Overland Park
KS 66210
Tel: (913) 345-0490
Fax: (913) 451-2443
Website:
http://www.gourmetgardener.com

More than 150 varieties of hard-to-find herbs, vegetable, and edible flower seeds from worldwide sources. All varieties are primarily selected for flavor, and the range includes a wide number of European heirloom varieties.
◆ Ships worldwide.
● Free catalog.

Greenseeds
Underwood Gardens, Ltd
4N381 Maple Avenue
Bensenville
IL 60106
Tel: (630) 616-0268
Fax: (630) 616-0232

Mother and daughter-run seed company, dedicated to conserving and supplying hard-to-find open-pollinated and heirloom seeds, including many rare and endangered species. Membership entitles supporters to the widest choice of seeds, but general catalog is available to all.
● Catalog $1.00.

Gurneys Received
Gurney's Seed and Nursery Company
110 Capital Street
Yankton
SD 57079

Huge selection of hardy vegetable seeds, including heirlooms.
● Free catalog.

Halifax
Halifax Seed Co Ltd
PO Box 8026
Station A
Halifax
Nova Scotia B3K 5L8
Canada

Seeds for maritime areas.
◆ Ships to Canada only.
● Catalog $1.00.

Heirloom Garden Seeds
PO Box 138
Guerneville
CA 95446

Rare and historic culinary and medicinal plant seeds.
● Catalog $2.50.

Heirloom
Heirloom Seeds
PO Box 245
West Elizabeth
PA 15088-0245
Tel: (412) 384-7816

Small family-run business supplying untreated open-pollinated seeds of heirloom vegetable and flower varieties, many dating from the 18th century.
◆ Ships worldwide.
● Catalog $1.00 refundable on first order.

Heritage Farm
see **Seed Savers Exchange**

Heritage
Heritage Seed Co
HC78 Box 187
Star City
AR 71667

Heirloom *Alliums* (flowers and vegetables) organically grown. Specialty onion list.
◆ Ships within US (including Hawaii and Alaska).
● Free catalog.

HighAlt
High Altitude Gardens
see also **Seeds Trust**
High Altitude Gardens
PO Box 1048
Hailey
ID 83333-1048
Tel: *catalog requests*
(208) 788-4363
queries and orders (208) 788 4419
Fax: (208) 788-3452
email: higarden@micron.net
Website:http://trine.com/Garden Net/higarden.htm

Family-run bioregional seed company, growing open-pollinated seeds adapted to cold short seasons, all tested at 6,000 feet – most do very well at low altitudes too. As well as a wide variety of vegetables, they also sell elusive wildflowers and native gasses.
◆ Ships seed worldwide.
● Catalogs include classics and heirlooms lists – send large SASE.
see also page 182

HortEnts
Horticultural Enterprises
PO Box 810082
Dallas
TX 75381-0082

Wide range of specialty chiles and Mexican vegetable varieties.
◆ Ships to US only.
● Free pricelist.

Howe
Howe Sound Seeds
PO Box 109
Bowen Island
British Columbia VON 1GO
Canada
Tel: (604) 947-0943
Fax: (604) 947-0945

Specializes in open-pollinated late-Victorian varieties from Europe.
● Catalogue $1.00.

Le Jardin du Gourmet
PO Box 75
St Johnsbury Center
VT 05863
Tel: (802) 748-1446
Fax: (802) 748-9592

Seeds for gourmet vegetables and herbs from around the world, including a specialty shallot collection.
● Free catalog.

JLH
J L Hudson, Seedsman
PO Box 1058
Redwood City   *Received*
California 94064
                    Added   2/24/99
One of the most interesting catalogs of any seed supplier, J L Hudson supplies untreated seeds of rare and unusual plants, and conducts ethnobotanical research. The catalog includes essays, booklists and general information as well as an incredibly wide selection of flower and vegetable seeds, including many rare and endangered species, and a good selection of traditional and heirloom vegetable varieties.
◆ Ships to US and Canada.
● Catalog $1.00, rare seed supplement 50c.

Johnnys
Johnny's Selected Seeds
310 Foss Hill Road
Albion
ME 04910
Tel: (207) 437-4301
Fax: (207) 437-9294

Catalog of organically grown seed includes a number of heirloom varieties, selected for flavor, productivity and adaptability. Most seed is untreated.
◆ Ships to US and Canada.
● Free catalog.

Kalmia
Kalmia Farm
PO Box 3881
Charlottesville
VA 22903

An interesting collection of heirloom multiplier onions, particularly potato onions, plus shallots and garlic varieties.
● Free catalog.

Kitazawa
Kitazawa Seed Co
1111 Chapman Street
San Jose
CA 95126

Specialist in Oriental vegetables since 1917.
● Free pricelist.

Landis
Landis Valley Heirloom Seed Project
Landis Valley Museum
2451 Kissel Hill Road
Lancaster
PA 17601
Tel: (717) 569-0402

Specializes in open-pollinated vegetable seed with Pennsylvanian historic connections – largely heirloom seed brought over with German immigrants pre-1940.
● Catalog $2.00 Canada, $2.75 US.

Landreth
D Landreth Seed Co
180-188 W Ostend Street
PO Box 6426
Baltimore
MD 21230
Tel: (410) 727-3922
Fax: (410) 244-8633

The oldest seed company in the US, founded in 1784, **Landreth** offers a large list of vegetables including a number of open-pollinated heirloom varieties.
● Catalog $2.00.

Ledden
Orol Ledden and Sons
PO Box 7
Sewell
NJ 08080
Tel: (609) 468-1000
Fax: (609) 464-0947

Open-pollinated heirlooms feature among many varieties on this commercial list.
● Free catalog.

Ledgerwood
Charles B Ledgerwood
3862 Carlsbad Boulevard
Carlsbad
CA 92008
Tel: (619) 729-3282

Specializes in varieties adapted to sub-tropical climate.
● Catalog $2.00.

Liberty
Liberty Seed Co
PO Box 806
New Philadelphia
OH 44663-0806
Tel: (330) 364-1611
Fax: (330) 364-6415

Some open-pollinated heirloom varieties are offered by this seed company, who have trial flower and vegetable gardens which are open to the public.
● Free catalog.

MacFayden
MacFayden Seeds
PO Box 1800
Brandon
Manitoba R7A 6N4
Canada
Tel: (204) 725-7300
◆ Ships to Canada only.
● Free catalog.

Mellinger's Inc
2310 W South Range Road
North Lima
OH 44452
Tel: (216) 549-9861
Fax: (216) 549-3716

Unusual and imported varieties of
vegetables, trees, and herbs.
● Catalog free to US.

Meyer
Meyer Seed Co
600 S Caroline St
Baltimore
MD 21231
Tel: (410) 342-4224
Fax: (410) 327-1469

Some open-pollinated and
heirloom varieties are offered
among the seeds supplied by this
old-established company.
● Free catalog.

Monticello
Thomas Jefferson Center for
Historic Plants
PO Box 316
Charlottesville
VA 22902
Tel: (804) 984-9860
Website:
http://www.monticello.org

The Center collects, preserves, and
sells historic plant varieties which
would have been grown by
Thomas Jefferson in his gardens at
Monticello. These gardens are
open to the public. All varieties
are documented as existing before
the 20th century, and the Center
also supplies the seed of some
varieties of indigenous Native
American plants.
◆ Ships to Canada and US only.
● Seedlist $1.00 (principally heir-
loom flowers, a few vegetables)
Newsletter $2.00.

Moose
see **Fedco Seeds and Moose Tubers**

Native
Native Seeds/SEARCH
2509 N Campbell Ave #325
Tucson
AZ 85719
Tel: (520) 327-9123
Fax: (520) 327-5821

Non-profit group working to conserve traditional crops, seeds, and
farming methods of the US
Southwest and Northern Mexico.
Native Seeds/SEARCH promotes
the use of native plants and their
wild relatives and works to
preserve knowledge about their
uses through research, training,
and community education.
Supplies limited quantities of
seeds of ancient crops and their
wild relatives suited to desert
environs. Native Seeds/SEARCH has
a demonstration garden in the
grounds of the Tucson Botanical
Gardens.
◆ Ships worldwide.
● Catalog $1.00.
see also page 182

Nichols
Nichols Garden Nursery
1190 North Pacific Highway
Albany
OR 97321-4580
Tel: (541) 928-9280
Fax: (503) 967-8406
Website:
http://www.pacificharbor.com
email: nichols@gardennursery.com

Herb and vegetable selection
features new and unusual vegetables, rare and gourmet varieties.
● Free catalog.

OldStur
Old Sturbridge Village
One Old Sturbridge Village Road
Sturbridge
MA 01566
Tel: (508) 347-3362
Fax: (508) 347-5375

Educational outdoor history
museum. Vegetable and flower
gardens demonstrate gardening
practices and styles of 1830s. Seeds
of early 19th century heirloom
varieties are available.
● Catalog and information $1.00.

The Onion Man
Mark McDonough
30 Mt Lebanon Street
Pepperell
MA 01463

Rare name *Allium* species.
● Free pricelist.

Ontario Seed Company
PO Box 144
Waterloo
Ontario N2J 3Z9
Tel: (519) 886-0557

Untreated open-pollinated
heirloom seeds.
◆ Ships to Canada only.
● Free catalog.

OrnEd
Ornamental Edibles
Specialty Seeds by Mail
3622 Weedin Court
San Jose
CA 95132
Tel: (408) 946-7333

A selection of open-pollinated
vegetable, herb, and edible flower
seeds from all round the world.
● Catalog $2.00.

Pepper Gal
PO Box 23006
Fort Lauderdale
FL 33307
Tel: (305) 537-5540
Fax: (305) 566-2208

Hot, sweet, and ornamental
peppers.
● Catalog $1.00.

Pepper Joe's
1650 Pembrooke Road
Noristown
PA 19403

Hot peppers, all seeds are grown
organically.
● Catalog free with SASE.

Peters Seed & Research
407 Maranatha Lane
Myrtle Creek
OR 97457
Tel/fax: (503) 863-3693

Independent seed and research business dedicated to preserving and improving rare plant varieties. Open-pollinated seed of specialty vegetables, large tomato collection, perennial grains. Supporting members have wider choice of seed.
Ships to US and Canada.
● Catalog $2.00.
see also page 182

Pinetree
Pinetree Garden Seeds
Box 300
New Gloucester
ME 04260
Tel: (207) 926-3400
Fax: (207) 926-3886

Catalog includes many interesting open-pollinated heirloom varieties – all varieties are selected above all for the home gardener with flavor in mind.
● Free catalog.

Ned W Place
21600 Conant Road
Wapakoneta
OH 45895
Tel: (419) 657-6727

Untreated and hand sorted seed of open-pollinated corn varieties.
● Free pricelist.

PlantsSW
Plants of the Southwest
RT 6
Box 11a
Santa Fe
NM 87501-9806
Tel: (505) 471-2212
Fax: (505) 438-8800

Southwestern native plants, corn, cover crops, and vegetables for arid gardens.
● Catalog $3.50.

Prairie
Prairie Grown Garden Seeds
Jim Ternier
Box 118
Cochin
Saskatchewan SOM 0LO
Canada
Tel: (306) 386-2737

A broad selection of older varieties of herbs, vegetables, grains, and wildflowers, suitable for growing in the Prairies without irrigation, as well as those suitable for other cool climate areas. Seeds are organically grown.
◆ Ships worldwide.
● Catalog $1.00 in US, $2.00 outside US.

Redwood
The Redwood City Seed Company
PO Box 361
Redwood City
CA 94064
Tel: (412) 325-7333

Aims to preserve the cultivated plant heritage of indigenous peoples worldwide and purchases seed directly from such growers where possible.
◆ Ships seed worldwide; bulbs and roots to US only.
● Catalog $1.00.

Rispens
Martin Rispens & Son
PO Box 5
Lansing
IL 60438

Large list includes open-pollinated heirloom vegetable varieties.
● Free catalog.

Rohrer
P L Rohrer & Bro Inc
PO Box 250
Smoketown
PA 17576
Tel: (717) 229-2571
Fax: (717) 229-5347

Commercial list includes open-pollinated heirloom varieties.
● Free catalog.

Ronniger
Ronniger's Seed Potatoes
Star Route
Moyie Springs
ID 83845
Fax: (208) 267-3265

Family-run seed potato and vegetable farm, supplying the widest range of organically grown potatoes, and onions and cover crops. Heirloom potato varieties include some from Europe..
◆ Ships within US including Hawaii and Alaska.
● Catalog $1.00.

SaltSpring
Salt Spring Seeds
PO Box 444
Ganges
Salt Spring Island
British Columbia V8K 2WI
Canada
Tel: (604) 537-5269

Supplies organically grown untreated seed. Specializes in varieties adapted to northern climates but not readily available in Canada, especially beans, grains, and tomatoes. Some heirloom varieties. Aims to set up a database of seed performance in different areas.
◆ Ships seed throughout Canada and US (but not garlic).
● Catalog $2.00.

Sanctuary Seeds
2774 West 4th Avenue
Vancouver
British Columbia V6K 1R1
Canada
Tel: (604) 738-4300

Untreated vegetable and herb seeds.
◆ Ships to Canada and US.
● Catalog $1.00

SandHill
Sand Hill Preservation Center
1878 230th St
Calamus
IA 52729
Tel: (319) 246-2299

Young family-run company dedicated to preserving heirloom seeds and poultry. Over 99% of seeds sold are grown on the farm. Chemical sprays may be used on cucumber, squash, and melon only, all seeds are untreated, no transgenic varieties.
◆ Seeds shipped worldwide.
● Catalog $1.00.

Saskaberia Seeds
Stanley Zubrowski
PO Box 26
Prairie River
Saskatchewan S0E 1J0
Canada

Although no longer selling seeds via mail order Stanley Zubrowski will still supply hard-to-find tomato seeds from his huge range, all adapted to grow in short season climates.

SeedSuch
Seeds and Such
PO Box 196
West Linn
OR 97068

Chile peppers and heirloom tomatoes.
● Free pricelist.

SeedsBlum
Seeds Blum
Idaho City Stage
Boise   *order 2/27/99*
ID 83706

Over 700 heirloom varieties are offered by one of the pioneers of the heirloom revival. All seeds are untreated and organically grown.
● Catalog $2.00.

Seedschange
Seeds of Change
PO Box 15700
Santa Fe
NM 87506-5700
Tel: (505) 438-8080
Fax: (505) 438-7052
email: gardener@seeds of change.com
Website: www.seeds of change.com

Over 400 varieties of open-pollinated seed for vegetables, flowers, and herbs, including many heirloom varieties, produced organically. Aims to further awareness of sustainable agriculture techniques and socially responsible food production.
◆ Ships seed worldwide.
● Catalog $1.00.
see also **DeepDiv / Deep Diversity**

Semillas Solanas
Sunny Land Seeds
PO Box 385
Paradox
CO 81429
Tel: (970) 859-7248

Supplies seeds of a variety of introduced plants from Ecuador and Southwest US.
● Catalog $1.00 with large SASE.

Shepherds
Shepherd's Garden Seeds
6116 Highway 9
Felton
CA 95018
Tel: (408) 335-6910
Fax: (408) 335-2080

European seeds for home gardeners.
● Free catalog with SASE.

order 2/27/99

SSE
Seed Savers Exchange
3076 North Winn Road
Decorah
IA 52101
Tel: (319) 382-5990
Fax: (319) 382-5872

Non-profit organization preserving heirloom varieties. The initial and principal seed saving network in the US, SSE has a huge seed bank and a 170 acre farm, open to visitors, where heirloom varieties are grown out Seed Savers Publications publishes *Seed Savers Yearbook* annually, listing over 1,000 members and 12,000 varieties of seeds available directly from members.

Heritage Farm
Headquarters of the **Seed Savers Exchange,** this 170-acre farm grows 20,000 heirloom vegetable varieties organically for seed, plus 700 old-time apples and a collection of hardy grapes, as well as heirloom flowers and herbs.

SSI
Seed Savers International
Project run by **Seed Savers Exchange,** supporting a network of plant collectors in Eastern Europe and former Soviet Union.

For SSE membership details see also page 182

SeedsWest
Seeds West Garden Seeds
Leslie Campbell
317 14th Street NW
Albuquerque
NM 97104
Tel: (505) 242-7474
email: SeedsWest@ad.com
Website:
http://home.aol.com/seedswest

A good range of open-pollinated vegetable and herb seeds includes many heirlooms; they also provide an excellent traditional flower collection.
● Catalog $2.00.

Shumway
RH Shumway Seedsman
PO Box 1
Graniteville
SC 29829
Fax: (803) 663-9772

Open-pollinated varieties and seed
corn, this company reintroduces
several heirloom varieties every
season.
● Free catalog.

Silver Springs Nursery
HCR 62 Box 86
Moyie Springs
ID 83845
Tel: (208) 267-5753
Fax: (208) 267-5753

Exceptionally cold-hardy gourmet
garlics.
● SASE for pricelist.

SESE
Southern Exposure Seed Exchange
PO Box 170
Earlysville
VA 22936
Tel: (804) 973-4703
Fax: (804) 973-8717
Website:
http://www.southernexposure.com

Aims to promote seed saving and
exchange, ecological agriculture,
and reduction of energy use by
increasing reliance on locally
adapted varieties and regional
food production. Most seed grown
without pesticides, synthetic
fertilizers or herbicides. All
seeds are untreated.
Specialties include heirloom and
old-fashioned varieties, insect and
disease resistant varieties, open-
pollinated varieties. SESE
maintains a seed bank of
rare seeds.
◆ Ships to US and Canada only.
● Catalog $3.00.
see also **Seed Shares** TM*page 182*

SOregon
Southern Oregon Organics
1130 Tetherow Road
Williams
OR 97544
Tel: (503) 846-7173

Open-pollinated varieties grown
and processed without chemicals.
● Free catalog.

Steele
Steele Plant Co
212 Collins Street
Gleason
TN 38229
Tel (901) 648-5476
Specializes in sweet potatoes, but
also carries a range of other open-
pollinated vegetables.
● Free catalog.

Stokes
Stokes Seeds Inc
Box 548
Buffalo
NY 14240
Tel: (716) 695-6890
Fax: (716) 697-9649

2500 vegetable and flower
varieties include some open-
pollinated heirlooms.
● Free catalog.

Synergy
Synergy Seeds
PO Box 323
Orleans
CA 95556
Voicemail: (916) 321-3769

Homegrown heirlooms and open-
pollinated vegetables well adapted to Northern California's
Mediterranean climate, plus native
wildflowers, herbs, grasses, and
legumes. All seeds are organically
grown using sustainable farming
methods. Synergy Seeds also offer
a consulting service on sustainable
growing, and are establishing
Confluence Nature Farm, a CSA
dedicated to cultural, historic and
genetic preservation.
No phone or fax, but voicemail is
on 24 hours.
● Catalog free with SASE.

TerrEd
Terra Edibles
Box 63
Thomasburg
Ontario K0K 3H0
Canada

Open-pollinated, organically
grown vegetable and flower
seeds, originating from many
parts of the world. Specializes in
heirlooms, varieties with high
flavor or nutritive value, and
plants for limited space.
● Free catalog.

Territorial
Territorial Seed Co
PO Box 157
20 Palmer Avenue
Cottage Grove
OR 97424
Tel: (541) 942-9547
Fax: (541) 924-9881
Website: www.territorial-seed.com

Specializes in varieties for year-
round food production in
Northern climates, produces a
special catalog for winter gardening. Most seed is untreated.
◆ Ships worldwide.
● Free catalog.

ThoMo
Thompson & Morgan
Dept 181-3
PO Box 1308
Jackson
NJ 08527
Tel: (908) 363-2225
Fax: (908) 363-9356

Selection of 3000 vegetable and
flower seeds, including rare and
exotic varieties, many from
Europe.
◆ Ships worldwide.
● Free catalog.

Threshold
Threshold Seeds Inc
Box 701
Claverack
NY 12513
Tel: (518) 672-5509

Non-profit corporation that produces, develops, and distributes
farm-based biodynamic seeds and
plant stocks. Subscription $20.00
for newsletter and priority orders.
Sells seed to home-gardeners and
non-subscribers.
● Catalog $2.00.
see also page 181

TomGro
Tomato Growers Supply
Company
PO Box 2237
Fort Myers
FL 33902
Tel: (941) 768-1119
Fax: (941) 768-3476

285 varieties of tomato, including
heirlooms, and 100 varieties of
pepper. Most seed is untreated.
● Free catalog.

ToTo
Totally Tomatoes
PO Box 1626
Augusta
GA 30903

Wide range of tomatoes, and
peppers.
● Free catalog.

Turtle
Turtle Tree Farm Seeds
5569 North County Road 29
Loveland
CO 80538

Biodynamic seed, mostly grown on
the farm. Open-pollinated
vegetable and flower varieties,
including some heirlooms. All seed
is hand cleaned.
● Catalog $1.00 donation invited.
see also page 181

Verbean
Vermont Bean Seed Co
Garden Lane
Fair Haven
VT 05743 0250
Tel: (802) 273-3400
Fax: (803) 663-9772

Believed to hold the world's
largest selection of beans and
peas; also French and Oriental vegetables. All seeds are untreated.
◆ Ships worldwide.
● Free catalog.

Weeks
Chris Weeks Peppers
PO Box 3207
Kill Devil Hills
NC 27948

One-man business grows and
supplies a great range of peppers.
● Free catalog.

Willhite
Willhite Seed Inc
PO Box 23
Poolville
TX 76487
Tel: (800) 828-1840
Fax: (817) 599-5843

Catalog includes special selections
of French and Indian vegetables;
large selection of melons and
watermelons.
● Free catalog.

Wood
Wood Prairie Farm
The Maine Potato Catalog
RFD1 Box 164
Bridgewater
ME 04735
Tel: (207) 429-9765
Orders (800) 829-9765
Fax (800) 300-6494

Organic vegetable farm supplying
scores of varieties of certified
organic seed potatoes, and some
other vegetable varieties.
◆ Ships to US only (including
Hawaii and Alaska).
● Catalog free with large SASE.

SEED SAVING NETWORKS & ORGANIZATIONS

Many independent seed suppliers offer their own membership schemes, seed exchanges and seed saving networks. The list below does not aspire to be comprehensive, but offers a number of useful starting points.

**Abundant Life
World Seed Fund**
see page 170

Established World Seed Fund in 1985 to send seeds to impoverished communities world-wide. Committed to supporting sustainable agriculture and empowering people to grow their own food. All seeds are open-pollinated, many are organically grown or wildcrafted.Every $25.00 donated to WSF could enable a family of six to plant a garden and eat for a year.
Membership: $30.00
Supporting $100.00
Sustaining.$500.00

BioDynamic Association
PO Box 550
Kimberton
PA 19442

Information on biodynamic agri-culture, and Stella Natura planting calendar.

BioDynamic Seed Initiative
contact
• **Aurora** *see page 171*

• **Threshold Seeds** *see page 180*

• **Turtle Tree Farm Seeds** *see page 180*

• **Elixir Botanicals (Medicinal Plant Seed)** Brixey, M0 65618

• **Corn Club (open-pollinated corn research),**
Michael Fields,
Agricultural Institute, W 2493
County Road ES,
East Troy, WI 53120

Butterbrooke Farm Co-op
see page 171

Seed Exchange and membership scheme. Membership entitles 20% discount on seeds, quarterly newsletter *Germinations*, and gardening advice.
Membership: Associate $12.50
Supporting $25.00
Lifetime £250.00.

**CSANA
Community Supported Agriculture of North America**
Robyn van En
CSA Indian Line Farm
RR3 Box 85
Great Barrington
MA 01230

Clearing house of information and assistance for existing and aspiring CSAs. Publishes *Basic Formula to Create CSA* @ $10.00.

Eastern Native Seed Conservancy
CRESS Heirloom Seed Conservation Project
PO Box 451
Great Barrington
MA 01230

CRESS is a regional seed exchange specializing in heirloom varieties that originate in, or are acclima-tized to, western New England and eastern New York State. Many varieties are also adaptable to other growing areas in the Northeast. Members receive an annual seed list .
Membership: $18.00.

ECHO Seed Sales
17430 Durrance Road
North Fort Myers
FL 33917-2239
Tel: (941) 543-3246
Fax: (941) 543-5317
email: echo@xc.org
Website: www.xc.org/echo

ECHO (Educational Concerns for Hunger Organization) is a non-profit Christian organization with a seed bank for under-utilized tropical plants. Seeds are supplied free to overseas development workers. Small amounts of seed sold to others. All seeds are treated with insecticide and fungicide, only suitable for subtropical regions.

Garden State Heirloom Seed Society
PO Box 15
Delaware
NJ 07833

Seed savers organization and seed exchange.
Membership $7.00.

Garlic Seed Foundation
Rose Valley FarmRose
NY 14542

Members receive an irregular newsletter with garlic events, news from members, reviews, research updates, and titbits.
Membership: £10.00.

KUSA Research Foundation
Non-profit organization dedicated to saving rare and endangered cereal crops.
Seed list: $2.00 + large SASE.

Maine Seed Saving Network
PO Box 126
Penobscot
ME 04476

Seed exchange and information.
Membership: Individual $8.00
Family $12.00.

Native Seeds/SEARCH
see page 176

Members receive 10% discount on
all purchases and workshops, and
quarterly newsletter *The Seedhead
News*. Dedicated to the preserva-
tion of endangered native plants,
and to redistributing native crops,
NSS hold various events at their
trial gardens throughout the year.
Membership: $20.00
Family $35.00
Low income $12.00
Free to Native Americans.

Peters Seed and Research
see page 177

Supporting membership scheme
provides access to unique open-
pollinated varieties, breeding ser-
vices, gene bank, and invitations
to trial grounds.
Membership: Home gardeners
$5.00; commercial growers and
seed companies $20.00.

Scatterseed Project
Box 1167
Farmington
ME 04938

Regional seed exchange, serving as
curator for part of SSE collection.

Seed Savers Exchange
see page 178

Membership includes an annual
copy of the *Seed Savers
Yearbook*,with the addresses of
more than 1,000 members, and
12,000 listings of rare and unusual
vegetable seeds.
Membership: US $25.00
Canada/Mexico $30.00
Overseas $40.00.

Seeds of Diversity Canada
Formerly **Heritage Seed Program**
Box 36
Station Q
Toronto
ONM4T 2L7

Membership scheme and seed
exchange programs, founded by
the Canadian Organic Growers in
1984, dedicated to preserving heirloom and endangered flowers,
vegetables, herbs and grains.
Members receive a quarterly
magazine and annual seed listing.
Membership: $18.00
Low income $15.00.

Seeds Trust
High Altitude Gardens
see page 174

Seeds Trust encourages and teach-
es seed saving, with programs and
lectures.

Southern Exposure Seed Exchange
Seed Shares™
see page 175

Seed exchange and gardeners'
seed bank for rare, endangered
and heirloom varieties.
Seed list: $1.00.

Arche Noah
Ober Strasse 40
3553 Schloss Schiltern
AUSTRIA
Tel: (0)2734 8626
Fax: (0)2734 8627

Arche Noah was established as a
seed saving network in the early
1990s, as a response to the decline
in local plant breeding and seed
production, and the disappearance
of many regionally adapted varieties. It now has around 2500
members, and maintains over 3500
plant varieties, including many
vegetables. About 1000 varieties
are grown out every year in their
Preservation gardens.
Arche Noah produce a yearly catalogue offering seed, and members
receive a newsletter. Arche Noah
also cooperates with **SSI** *see page
178.*

**Henry Doubleday Research
Association (HDRA)**
Heritage Seed Library
Genetic Resources Department
Ryton Organic Gardens
Ryton-on-Dunsmore, Coventry,
CV8 3LG
Tel: 01203 303517
Fax: 01203 639229
Email: enquiry@hdra.org.uk

HDRA is Europe's main campaigning organization to preserve diversity. It established its Seed Library
in 1975 in response to the threat
to vegetable varieties posed by
European legislation. Stocks of
around 600 varieties are
maintained at HDRA and by Seed
Guardians around the country
who are each responsible for one
or several varieties. Each year
members of the Heritage Seed
Library receive three newsletters,
and a catalog containing a selection of Seed Library varieties from
which they can obtain free seeds.
The catalog includes a Seed Swap
Register, enabling members to
exchange seeds.
HDRA campaign nationally, and in
Europe, on issues concern genetic
diversity. Their publications include
the *Fruit and Vegetable Finder*
which lists legally available
varieties and their sources.

FURTHER READING

GENERAL REFERENCE

Gardening for Profit, including *Garden and Farm Topics*
Peter Henderson, original editions 1867, 1884, facsimile edition 1991, The
American Botanist, $20.00
Peter Henderson was a Scottish immigrant who became a truck farmer in
New Jersey, and revealed scores of secrets for small farm success, many of
whch are as true today as they were then.

The Vegetable Garden
Vilmorin-Andrieux, originally published in 1885, facsimile reprint of
English edition, 1981, Ten Speed Press, $20.00
The classic reference work, with details of thousands of varieties of
vegetables available in Europe at the end of the 19th century.

Edible Plants of the World
J.P.Sturtevant, ed U.P.Hedrick, 1972, Dover, $20.00
Originally published in 1919, this invaluable reference work gives detailed
biological information about edible plants throughout the world, including
origins, and growing conditions.

Shattering - food politics and the loss of genetic diversity
Cary Fowler and Pat Mooney, 1990, University of Arizona Press, $17.95
Required reading for those concerned with the future of gardening and the
planet. Compelling arguments by two influential agricultural activists as to
why we must conserve varieties and save our own seeds.

Seed Savers Exchange: The First Ten Years
Kent Whealy and Arllys Adelmann (eds), Seed Saver Publications (*see Seed
Savers Exchange page 178*), $16.00
The best articles from 10 years of membership publications. This book is
a fascinating look back at the growth of the largest grassroots genetic
preservation movement in the US.

Seeds of Change: The Living Treasure
Ken Ausubel, 1994, Harper Collins
This inspiring book discusses the passionate story of the growing
movement to restore biodiversity and to raise public awareness of the
issues surrounding genetic diversity.

SEEDS

Seed to Seed
Suzanne Ashworth, 1991, Seed Saving Publications (*Seed Savers Exchange, see page 178*) $20.00
The most complete seed saving guide for 160 crops. Invaluable reference for beginners or experienced seed savers.

Growing Garden Seeds
A Manual for Gardeners and Small Farmers
Robert Johnston, 1983, Johnny's Selected Seeds (*see page 173*) $2.50
Indispensable no-nonsense guide to seed production, saving, and storage of the 40 commonest vegetable crops. Perfect for beginners.

Saving Seeds
Marc Rogers, 1991, Garden Way Publishing, $12.95
Gardeners' guide to growing and storing flower and vegetable seeds.

Garden Seed Inventory   ordered 2/27/99
Seed Saver Publications (*see Seed Savers Exchange page 178*) $22.00
Comprehensive inventory of US and Canadian mail-order seed catalogs, the essential guide to suppliers of all open-pollinated vegetable seeds. Use this guide to locate endangered seeds, buy them, and save the seed!

Seeds, the Definitve Guide to Growing, History and Lore
Peter Loewer, Macmillan Reference, $25.00
A look at the vast and complex world of seeds, including how-to grow all kinds of plants from seed, and a discussion of the role of seeds in history.

HEIRLOOM VEGETABLE GARDENING

Taylor's Guide to Heirloom Vegetables
Benjamin Watson, 1996, Houghton Mifflin, $20.00
A comprehensive illustrated guide to 500 historic varieties, including instructions on how to select and grow the best heirlooms for your garden.

Heirloom Vegetable Gardening   Purchased 3/14/99 for $25.01
William Woys Weaver, 1997, Henry Holt & Co, $45.00
Weaver focuses on 280 varieties of 37 vegetables in this encyclopedic guide to some of America's treasured heirloom vegetables.

Heirloom Gardens: Simple secrets for old-fashioned flowers and vegetables
Mimi Luebbermann, 1997, Chronicle, $14.95
Basic tips to get you started on heirloom gardening.

GENERAL GARDENING

Four Season Harvest
Eliot Coleman, 1992, Chelsea Green, $19.95
Gardeners in cold climates have traditionally closed up their gardens in September, relying on root cellar and freezer for winter supplies. But this book escapes the confines of short cold growing seasons; it describes how to plan the outside garden, planting and cultivation, using cold frames, tunnel greenhouses, and root cellars.

Organic Gardening in Cold Climates
Sandra Perrin, 1991, Mountain Press, $10.00
Direct, concise, and practical guide, beginning with the unworked soil and ending with saving the seeds, covering everything in between.

Warm Climate Gardening
Barbara Pleasant, 1993, Harper Collins, $12.95
Solutions to gardening successfully in excessive and prolonged heat, as well as ways to enjoy the garden in cooler months.

The Small Ecological Garden
Sue Stickland, 1996, Arthur Schwartz & Co, $15.95
Everything beginners and experts need to know to create a healthy organic garden in limited space – including soil care, choice of plants, cultivation techniques, design suggestions and encouraging garden wildlife.

The New Organic Grower: A Master's Manual of Tools and Techniques for the Home and Market Gardener
Eliot Coleman, 1996
Recently updated and expanded comprehensive manual, including chapter on organic pest management.

How to Grow More Vegetables
John Jeavons, 1995, Ten Speed Press, $16.95
The bible of bio-intensive gardening – 325,000 copies in print worldwide. Contains detailed charts of individual vegetables, precise garden layouts. complete information on companion planting, compost and fertilizers.

Food from Dryland Gardens
David Cleveland and Daniela Soleri, 1991, Center for People, $25.00
An excellent tool for low-input, sustainable gardening where water is limited. It provides plenty of examples of traditional methods from the world's drylands.

The Salad Garden
Joy Larkcom, 1991, reprinted 1996, Penguin/Viking, $18.95
Gardening techniques and information about every salad green, from the commonest to the less well-known, native, European, and Oriental. Helpful for beginners and experienced gardeners.

The Pepper Garden
Dave de Witt and Paul W. Bosland, 1993, Ten Speed Press, $12.95
This is the pepper growers' bible! It takes readers right through the growing process and includes fascinating titbits of history. A must for all chile aficionados!

Growing Great Garlic
Ron Engeland, 1995, Filaree Productions (*see Filaree Farm, page 173*), $12.95
All you need to know to grow great garlic – the author raises over 200 distinct strains.

Blue Potatoes, Orange Tomatoes
Rosalind Creasy, 1994, Sierra Club Books, $15.95
Lively illustrated book for young gardeners, with everything they need to know to grow a whole cornnucopia of fruits and vegetables. Includes garden planning, preparing the soil and planting and cultivating organically.

Weeds and What they Tell
EE Pfeiffer, classic work reprinted and available from Abundant Life Seed Foundation (*see page 170*) $4.50 + $1.00 pp.
The basic reference for intrepreting soils by the types of plant they support.

Carrots love Tomatoes – secrets of companion planting for successful gardening
Louise Riotte, 1986, Garden Way, $11.95
Guide to fruit and vegetables' natural friends and enemies – for example, beans and onions are natural enemies, but carrots and beans will grow happily together.

Carrots really detest tomatoes
Craig Dremann, 1992, $2.50 postpaid from Redwood Seeds (*see page 177*)
This booklet is based on the results of one seed company's tests, showing their remarkable results as to who the real companions were and who were the antagonists.

INDEX

Entries in **bold** refer to **Directory** entries; numerals in *italic* refer to illustrations.